CRYPTOCURRENCY

FROM BLOCKCHAIN AND **BITCOIN** TO **ALTCOINS** AND **CRYPTOCURRENCY EXCHANGES**, YOUR ESSENTIAL GUIDE TO **UNDERSTANDING**, **ACQUIRING**, AND **USING CRYPTOCURRENCY** 101

JOE DUARTE, MD

Adams Media

New York Amsterdam/Antwerp London Toronto Sydney/Melbourne New Delhi

Adams Media
An Imprint of Simon & Schuster, LLC
100 Technology Center Drive
Stoughton, MA 02072

For more than 100 years, Simon & Schuster has championed authors and the stories they create. By respecting the copyright of an author's intellectual property, you enable Simon & Schuster and the author to continue publishing exceptional books for years to come. We thank you for supporting the author's copyright by purchasing an authorized edition of this book.

First Adams Media hardcover edition
April 2026

Simon & Schuster strongly believes in freedom of expression and stands against censorship in all its forms. For more information, visit BooksBelong.com.

For information about special discounts for bulk purchases, please contact Simon & Schuster Special Sales at 1-866-506-1949 or business@simonandschuster.com.

The Simon & Schuster Speakers Bureau can bring authors to your live event. For more information or to book an event, contact the Simon & Schuster Speakers Bureau at 1-866-248-3049 or visit our website at www.simonspeakers.com.

Manufactured in the United States of America

1 2026

Library of Congress Control Number: 2025949136

ISBN 978-1-5072-2596-7
ISBN 978-1-5072-2597-4 (ebook)

Many of the designations used by manufacturers and sellers to distinguish their products are claimed as trademarks. Where those designations appear in this book and Simon & Schuster, LLC, was aware of a trademark claim, the designations have been printed with initial capital letters.

This publication is designed to provide accurate and authoritative information with regard to the subject matter covered. It is sold with the understanding that the publisher is not engaged in rendering legal, accounting, or other professional advice. If legal advice or other expert assistance is required, the services of a competent professional person should be sought.
—From a *Declaration of Principles* jointly adopted by a Committee of the American Bar Association and a Committee of Publishers and Associations

CONTENTS

INDEX   281

INTRODUCTION

Cryptocurrency is a fascinating and expansive financial landscape. Each day, more and more people are curious about how they can make money within this exciting and ever-changing market. If you've ever been intrigued by this new, complex world—whether it's learning about these currencies' many types, understanding how to use coins as a form of payment, navigating regulations, or getting the right gear to mine it—then this book will help you navigate this unique market and set you up for financial success.

In *Cryptocurrency 101*, you'll get the most up-to-date information about all aspects of these digital currencies, which will allow you to diversify your investment portfolio to include more than stocks and bonds. You'll learn that trading crypto may be a better bet than mining for it, and how crypto shifts with the supply and demand of the market around it. Throughout this book, you'll learn more about this currency, including:

- How to invest in crypto for the long and short term.
- How essential blockchains are for keeping track of crypto.
- How external factors like interest rates may affect your crypto holdings.
- How to use the consistency of stablecoins as a solid diversification method for your portfolio.

- How to leverage your investment portfolio by including crypto-related assets.
- And more!

This book will explain what cryptocurrency is, how to use and mine it on a computer, and the intricacies of trading it. You'll learn the difference between hot and cold wallets, solo mining and pool mining, and Bitcoin versus the other players in the crypto space. All it takes to have monetary success with crypto is a bit of knowledge, insight, discipline, and flexibility. With a little time and practice, you'll be able to pick the right currencies to invest in, understand and follow the state and federal tax laws that apply to cryptocurrency, and start making profits.

However you decide to enter the world of these digital currencies, *Cryptocurrency 101* will assist you with your goal to learn more about making money with this ever-growing financial vehicle. Let's get started.

Chapter 1

The Fundamentals of Cryptocurrency

The term "currency" can be defined as a method of value storage and exchange through which transactions are made for goods and services. For example, when you buy a loaf of bread for a dollar, you give the store owner the dollar and the store owner gives you the loaf of bread, with the understanding that the dollar and the loaf of bread are valued equally, making the exchange fair and true. Until the development of digital currencies, the only way to exchange value via money was through physical means (cash, for example). Through the advent of digital currencies, including crypto, transactions are now possible at the click of a mouse or a computer key without the need for physical money.

The cryptocurrency space is large and still growing, but Chapter 1 provides the fundamentals. Throughout this chapter, you'll learn about what a cryptocurrency is and how it came to be. You'll dive into more crypto terminology, like blockchains, and even learn how to utilize and differentiate types of crypto. Finally, you'll learn about privacy coins and the very basics of trading and investing in crypto.

WHAT IS CRYPTOCURRENCY?

A Type of Digital Currency

At its simplest, cryptocurrency is a vehicle to make payments or store value without government/banking interference. Crypto uses cryptography (coded letters and numbers) to keep transactions secure while existing on a decentralized finance (DeFi) blockchain network—a digital ledger/recordkeeping network where control and decision-making is distributed among its participants instead of a central authority. This gives cryptocurrency an unmatched level of security and transparency, which decreases the potential for fraud. Because nothing is linked to personal data, many cryptocurrencies are anonymous.

Cryptocurrency is a popular growing digital currency, and before you can understand crypto as a whole, you first need to understand what digital currency is. A digital currency (also called digital money, electronic money, electronic currency, or cybercash) is a nonphysical, electronic/digital currency that serves the same purpose as physical currency (cash). Digital currency is a way to store financial value, and it may be used to pay for goods and services, assuming the buyer and the seller agree on the price (e.g., the loaf of bread costs one unit/coin).

TRADITIONAL CURRENCY VERSUS DIGITAL CURRENCY

The big difference between physical (traditional) and digital currencies is that physical currencies are in our pockets and wallets, while digital currencies are in cyberspace. You can store digital currencies as data, never being able to really get a physical representation of it (like you can with a dollar bill).

However, as long as the two parties involved in a transaction agree that the exchange of the currency for the goods and services involved is legally binding, based on the legal tender principle, the transaction is valid. The legal tender principle is a promise from the issuing government that it will honor the currency it issues based solely on the promise that it will do so. Although you can make digital transactions using conventional currencies through credit card mediated means (buying products on Amazon.com, for example), a true digital currency shares specific qualities and differences from cryptocurrencies. For example:

- Both digital currencies and cryptocurrencies are accessible electronically, through computers or mobile phones.
- Digital currencies may be backed by governments and offer less anonymity and transaction privacy than cryptocurrencies. Cryptocurrencies are decentralized, meaning they don't require intermediaries such as the US Treasury, central or private banks to settle transactions. Cryptocurrencies are not legal tender unless they are explicitly designated to be so by individual governments, such as in the case of El Salvador.
- Both can ease international transactions when the two parties are connected to the same electronic network or exchange.
- There is a slow progression, which is steadily improving, to make cryptocurrencies legal tender, while more "official" government-backed digital currencies are evolving less rapidly.

Physical currency, meanwhile, does not meet these standards.

NOT ALL DIGITAL CURRENCIES
ARE CRYPTO

All cryptocurrencies and related variations on the theme are digital currencies, yet not all digital currencies qualify for the cryptocurrency category. The difference between digital currencies and cryptocurrencies is that while the former applies to any currency or asset that is viewed as money that trades electronically, cryptocurrencies are a specific type of digital currency that uses cryptography (encoded letters and symbols) and operates specifically on blockchain networks. Here are the defining characteristics of cryptocurrencies:

- They are cryptographically protected to maximize anonymity and privacy.
- They operate on DeFi platforms and you can use them for direct peer-to-peer transactions.
- Transactions are final and are recorded on blockchain networks (electronic ledgers).
- Groups of transactions are organized into blocks that are linked together (hence the name "blockchain").
- They exist digitally and are stored in digital wallets.
- Their value is determined by the status of the supply and demand for each coin.

In contrast, there are many government-backed, central bank–regulated digital coins at different stages of development. Generally, these are referred to as central bank digital currencies (CBDCs) and they should not be mistaken for cryptocurrencies. For example, the Chinese central bank (People's Bank of China, or

PBOC) is testing the digital yuan, while Sweden's Riksbank is working on the e-krona. The UK and the European Union are respectively exploring the creation of a digital pound (Britcoin) and a digital euro, while the Bank of Canada is looking at creating a digital Canadian dollar. For its part, the US Federal Reserve is also exploring the possibility of introducing a digital dollar. These digital currencies only share the digital medium as a common characteristic with cryptocurrencies. Furthermore, government-backed digital currencies are essentially digital forms of that government's own fiat currency (money that's issued by a centralized government), and thus are easily traceable—the opposite of what cryptocurrencies aim for.

Thus, the central difference between some of these digital currencies and crypto is clear: Government-backed digital currencies are just digital versions of the particular country's physical currency and are therefore backed by the legal tender promise of the issuing country. Again, a defining part of cryptocurrency is its lack of centralization—there are no countries "backing" their worth.

Transactions made with decentralized digital currencies, such as Bitcoin, are anonymous because they are not linked to personal data. This makes these coins attractive since they are somewhat protected from government scrutiny. So, cryptocurrencies not affiliated with governments, such as Bitcoin, have been widely accepted by large numbers of people, especially as an asset class (a group of investments that share similar characteristics, such as precious metals or technology stocks). Government-backed digital currencies, meanwhile, have faced a great deal of opposition from those who are concerned about the loss of privacy and government access to personal financial data.

ACQUIRING AND USING CRYPTO

You can acquire cryptocurrencies via crypto exchanges such as Binance, Coinbase, or Kraken or through specialized apps. The process is simple and requires opening an account, depositing your fiat currency (dollars, euros, pound sterling) and exchanging it for your desired cryptocurrency. For example, you can convert your dollars to bitcoin or ether (ETH) on an exchange and then store it in your wallet. You can also buy cryptocurrencies via peer-to-peer transactions on specialized platforms that cater to this type of transaction. The details for simple acquisition of cryptocurrencies are in Chapter 4.

A second way to obtain cryptocurrencies is through mining, a complex process which involves your computer competing with other computers to solve complex mathematical equations. The first computer to arrive at the solution receives cryptocurrency as a payment (reward) for solving the puzzle. The full details on the mining process are in Chapter 5.

Finally, you can also obtain cryptocurrencies indirectly by investing in exchange-traded funds (ETFs), which are specialized investment vehicles you get through your broker similar to how you buy and sell stocks. Learn all about crypto ETFs in Chapter 6.

Some Inflexibilities of Digital Currencies

One important point to keep in mind when using cryptocurrencies is that once the transaction is made, it's irreversible. There's no way to get the currency back if you've made a bad deal, or, unfortunately, if you're hacked.

BLOCKCHAIN EXPLAINED

The Bookkeeper of Crypto

Blockchain is the bookkeeping system of cryptocurrencies, although it's not exclusive to crypto. Blockchains are necessary for trading crypto while keeping anonymity—they're essential for keeping a user's information secure without the need of a central authority (bank) to be part of the picture. Think of blockchain as a database in which information is stored and shared between transacting computers. It keeps a secure and decentralized transaction record that requires the input of data by one party, reducing costs and the chances of errors.

Blockchain keeps records in blocks (a series of transactions that are recorded together on a blockchain), which are linked together by cryptography (a mathematical method for encrypting and decrypting data, also used in spycraft to keep communications secret from prying eyes). Moreover, what sets blockchain apart from other recordkeeping systems is that the data cannot be altered once it is entered. Plus, the Bitcoin blockchain is decentralized, allowing all users to control it collectively.

THE MECHANICS OF BLOCKCHAIN

Blockchain is made up of scripts, which preserve and store information entered during transactions. Multiple copies of each blockchain are distributed and stored on multiple computers within the network where the transaction took place. Each separately stored blockchain copy must match all others as a mismatch indicates either a potential error in the network or possible tampering, or else the chain is considered invalid. This failure in the blockchain authentication process is akin to what happens when there is faulty code on the Internet that leads to a connection error rendering a website inaccessible.

Bitcoin blockchain collects transaction data and organizes it into a 4-megabyte (MB) file known as a block, whose size differs based on the chain being used. Once the block is filled, it's run through a cryptographic hash function; this is a mathematical function that creates the block header hash (the large hexadecimal digit used to identify the transaction, for example 01000000 6fk28c0ab6f1b49x1a-6b246ae63f74f931e8365e15a089y75b4320000000000 964431fd1e4ba744bxxy75364xyz14677ba1a3c3540bf7b1cgy-06e857233e0e 61bc7703 ffff001d 01e36299 01. Each header hash is then encrypted and incorporated with existing blocks creating the blockchain.

The following discussion of block headers illustrates an important concept, but pertains exclusively to Bitcoin. Other cryptocurrencies may have similar but quite disctinctive components in their respective blockchain design. However, the overall purpose of blockchain remains the same; that of providing a permanent record of cryptocurrency transactions.

Block headers identify individual blocks in a chain and are used by Bitcoin developers to document their modification tasks on each blockchain and to build a history of the coin and its transactions. They also provide a "proof of work" used by miners for mining rewards. This is an integral part of keeping the blockchain running smoothly and efficiently.

Each Bitcoin block has three parts, while other cryptocurrencies may differ in their particular structure. The Bitcoin number (used in Bitcoin protocol) keeps track of the changes in the protocol. The second is the difficulty number, which measures how much computer power was required to mine the coin. The last is the nonce value, a randomly generated number used only once in the mining process, which ensures the security of the blockchain. The nonce is used to add a new block to the blockchain. It is a required part of the crypto mining puzzle and it requires multiple attempts by the miner to find the correct figure. The nonce number is increased by one for each failed attempt to find the one that matches.

Individual blocks contain three sets of block metadata along with multiple individual components. Each block is then vertically layered on top of the prior block, with the first block (also known as the "genesis block") serving as the base of the stack. This layering of blocks provides a complete history of the coin and is a key feature in making Bitcoin secure.

Complexity of Block Layering

A hash is a fixed set of characters generated by input into a blockchain and serves as an identifier for the input data. A sample of a hash for a block numbered 398765 looks like this: 000000000000000004fb5c6a6285e983e49eec2b74078b-5b0495a3cfe1bc7d25.

A BITCOIN TRANSACTION

A Bitcoin transaction has a particular flow, which is simplified here while documenting the major steps in the process. Once you initiate the process via tapping funds in your crypto wallet, your request is sent to a memory pool (a group of computers that solves equations to verify the validity of the transaction). Legitimate transactions are packaged into blocks that are then chained together. This creates a complete history of all permanent transactions involving this coin. Then the transaction is complete.

A complete transaction and the entire verification process takes about an hour because multiple computers are working on the process simultaneously. In contrast, Ethereum's transaction process involves only one computer whose validation is confirmed by the network.

ADDITIONAL BLOCKCHAIN INFORMATION

You can use special programs called blockchain explorers to watch any transaction as it occurs live. This allows the tracking of any bitcoin anywhere, and the transparency allows for tracking of hacked coins while the Bitcoin users remain anonymous.

Additionally, as new blocks are added to the chain, the prior blocks cannot be altered—all blocks are added to the chain linearly and chronologically. Thus, any block alteration is likely to lead to a rejection of the chain and related transactions. The fine print is that alteration is possible but difficult in smaller networks, making it nearly impossible in the Bitcoin network and highly unlikely in the Ethereum network.

Furthermore, blockchain can be adapted to almost any transaction-related process. This is important because blockchains may possibly be applied to elections in order to cut down fraud potential. Other targeted areas include banking, healthcare, maintaining property records in municipalities, and supply chain management. Major corporations such as Walmart, Visa, and Delta Air Lines are using blockchain in their business applications.

At the end of the day, however, there is always the potential for fraud, and the use of Bitcoin and other cryptocurrencies for illicit transactions on the dark web still exists. So, it pays to be fully informed and to transact your crypto business on the highest-rated platforms.

Blockchain in the Supply Chain

Blockchain is widely used in the supply chain. For example, it's part of the recordkeeping system used to monitor the transit of food from farmers to grocery stores. This is in case there's a need to pinpoint important developments, such as a specific point where product contamination may have occurred.

THE ORIGINS OF CRYPTOCURRENCY

Learning Crypto's Storied Past

The foundation of blockchain technology began with the 1982 publication of a paper by David Chaum cryptically titled "Computer Systems Established, Maintained, and Trusted by Mutually Suspicious Groups." This paper led to a chain of events resulting in the creation of Bitcoin, its competitors, and the expansion of the cryptocurrency space as a whole.

THE PAPER TRAIL

In his paper, Chaum described and proved how to send and receive digital tokens outside the purview and control of central authorities (such as governments and central banks) via the use of specialized encryption techniques. He followed it up with the creation of eCash, the first digital currency, which, unfortunately, ran out of steam in 1998 despite interest from the likes of Microsoft. But Chaum's concept of a digital currency was still influential. About a decade later, Satoshi Nakamoto (the pseudonym of Bitcoin's founder/founders) invented Bitcoin, the bellwether for decentralized cryptocurrency. Nakamoto reportedly modeled Bitcoin on the general characteristics of gold, and modeling gold's scarcity; the secretive founder crafted a limit of 21 million Bitcoins.

Nakamoto mined the first bitcoin in 2008 and the first recorded transaction involving Bitcoin was the purchase of a Papa John's pizza for 10,000 bitcoins (BTC), in 2009, which is why May 22 is celebrated by the Bitcoin crowd as "Bitcoin Pizza Day."

Bitcoin Lore

A central tenet of the Bitcoin lore is that Nakamoto had a deep distrust of centralized authority when he created the cryptocurrency. Thus, he designed Bitcoin as an alternative payment method to standard currencies through which participants could conduct business without the scrutiny of governments and central banks.

THE FIRST "PRICE PUMP"

Bitcoin's price history is an exercise in volatility as its value lingered below $1 until 2010–2011, when it erupted from below $0.60 to a high of $34. Much of the move took place in June 2011 prior to an eventual price regression to $2. Despite the impressive price jump, Bitcoin was perceived as a way to conduct illicit, "under the table" transactions. And although the public's perception has changed, in many circles, Bitcoin is still seen today as a "shady" method of payments, as we still see occasional instances where law enforcement uncovers illicit activity in which Bitcoin is involved.

CRYPTO'S GROWING PAINS

Trouble in the crypto space resurfaced in 2014 when the prominent crypto exchange, Mt. Gox, was hacked and 850,000 bitcoins were stolen. The hack resulted from poor security measures for guarding individual wallets. This resulted in improved security employed by current exchanges such as Binance and Coinbase.

The creation of the Bitcoin Foundation and *Bitcoin Magazine* in 2012 improved the image and adoption of Bitcoin as an authentic, working asset.

Overall, Bitcoin has proven to be a viable asset over time, especially as a trading vehicle. Moreover, it has spawned other related cryptocurrencies, especially stablecoins (cryptocurrencies that maintain value because they're pegged against other currencies or assets, like a dollar or silver), which are being steadily accepted as mainstream payment methods by major retailers including Shopify.com, Chipotle, and Whole Foods.

The Crypto Market's Worth

The entire cryptocurrency market is estimated to be worth over $3 trillion as of June 2025. The rapid growth is related to the creation of ETFs (trading vehicles with cryptocurrencies as the underlying asset) and the expansion of treasury companies (companies that invest in cryptocurrencies as part of their business strategies).

THE EXPANSION OF THE CRYPTO SPACE

In 2015, a new cryptocurrency emerged on the scene: Ethereum. Ethereum's designers aimed to enhance blockchain technology by implementing automated (self-executing) smart contracts. These contracts contain the terms and specific conditions to govern transactions. Kevin McCoy and Anil Dash created the first non-fungible token (Quantum) in 2014. Ethereum then standardized the use of NFTs on its blockchain in 2018 via the introduction of ERC-721. ERC-721 is the framework for token creation where no two are alike and have distinct attributes to differentiate from other tokens. This important development was similar to the creation of the DAO, a decentralized autonomous organization without centralized leadership that uses blockchain technology to manage operating decisions and finances through smart contracts.

Unfortunately, hackers broke into the DAO fund later in 2016 and stole $60 million of the total $150 million housed within it, causing a big upset. The result was a "forking," or a dividing up of the space with the creation of a new Ethereum, now the most widely used form of the cryptocurrency. The original "classic" Ethereum (Ethereum Classic) is still available, but it is less influential today.

THE BREAKOUT PHASE

Every investment reaches a point known as a "breakout," which is defined as a period of time when, after years of sideways move-ment, prices jump above a previously rejected level (a price level above which prices had not been able to rise before this period) and moved decidedly higher. The cryptocurrency space engineered its breakout starting in 2018, further becoming a highly sought-after asset after the pandemic in 2020.

The first significant move of cryptocurrency came in December 2017, when Bitcoin broke above $10,000 per coin and moved to $20,000. After this jump, Bitcoin entered a period of consolida-tion described by some as a "crypto winter." After a lot of volatil-ity, which was caused by a lot of changes in the space (such as the creation of new cryptos and the creation of other crypto-related products), the winter ended and the next phase erupted.

Another major milestone came in 2017, when the Chicago Mercantile Exchange (CME) began to offer Bitcoin futures. The Chicago Board Options Exchange (CBOE) offered the contracts as well, but eventually discontinued them. Bitcoin futures continue to trade on CME as of late 2025. Still, the fuse was lit as the initial stamp of legitimacy offered by a crypto-based futures contract did not go unnoticed.

In 2020, as the pandemic progressed and the Federal Reserve infused the financial system with trillions of newly created dollars, crypto flourished, partly fueled by day traders who had been confined to their homes by the pandemic. The price of one Bitcoin rocketed above $60,000 in April and November 2021 and eventually made it to $70,000 in the spring of 2024. Its all-time high clocked in above $125,000 in September 2025.

The period that has followed every dramatic new high is often very volatile with the price falling significantly before reversing. In 2025, Bitcoin routinely traded above $100,000 and became a "normal" trading and investment vehicle for countless traders and investors. Moreover, the creation and expansion of crypto-based exchange-traded funds (ETFs) has injected a new level of interest and liquidity into the space.

The Bybit Hacker Scandal

In February 2025, hackers infiltrated Bybit's multi-signature Ethereum wallet, getting away with $1.5 billion in crypto. The hack resulted from security vulnerabilities in Bybit's wallet infrastructure and was attributed to North Korea's Lazarus Group. The proceeds were then laundered, and the event triggered price volatility in both Ethereum and Bitcoin.

USES FOR CRYPTOCURRENCIES

Beyond Just Investing

While the main focus of this book is investing with cryptocurrency, it is important to understand the practical sides of crypto and its many uses. As crypto becomes more useful in the tangible world, the more likely it will be cemented as an investment and vice versa.

Cryptocurrencies were originally designed to be used for financial transactions; however, its potential uses have expanded into investing. The community side (the interactions on the blockchain of the collective participants) of crypto is often overlooked—when examined, this portion adds several layers of potential expansion for users. This includes the provision of support, sharing knowledge, and the collaboration between developers in order to enhance blockchain platforms. This entry explores a few of the unnoticed but easily deployed alternative uses for crypto.

ANONYMOUS FINANCIAL TRANSACTIONS

This may have been Nakamoto's primary design for Bitcoin: the ability to make financial transactions anonymously. Using and mining crypto helps you avoid bank and government scrutiny when you want to transfer large sums of money, for legitimate purposes, without delays. However, as more regulations are applied to crypto, the anonymity angle will likely be blurred. This decrease in anonymity will continue as more traditional banks enter the crypto space and as stablecoins gain ground, especially stable-coins backed by traditional fiat currencies, such as the US dollar and other government-linked treasury bonds/bills.

MONEY TRANSFERS

Instead of using bank-based, often slow-to-process money trans-fers, a crypto-based transaction may take only a few minutes. This process could be quite useful when trying to balance your books or make a competitive purchase. In addition, the low cost of the transaction (compared to bank fees for similar financial transfers) makes this alternative method attractive. Bitcoin Cash (BCH) is an example of an easy transferable cryptocurrency. Bitcoin Cash is separate from Bitcoin and was created by developers who were looking to speed up transaction time and the blockchain's capacity to conduct a larger number of transactions compared to the origi-nal Bitcoin blockchain.

LENDING CRYPTO FOR YIELD

Another overlooked use of cryptocurrencies is the practice of "yield farming," which refers to the process of lending your coins for a fee. In some cases, you may be able to collect 10%–12% annu-ally. That said, the practice of lending your coins for interest pay-ments is not risk-free. Some crypto-lending platforms have failed, resulting in clients losing all their money. Moreover, crypto is not insured by the Federal Deposit Insurance Corporation (FDIC), so your losses in these scenarios are permanent and irreversible.

SAFE STORAGE OF WEALTH

Crypto, although not risk-free, offers the potential for safety during politically volatile times, although much of the price action in cryptocurrencies depends on liquidity. Liquidity is the amount of money available in the financial system at any time and is primarily influenced by central banks. Generally speaking, periods where liquidity is ample are favorable for all financial markets. Certainly, daily price fluctuations in crypto can be gut-wrenching and are often based on seemingly random events, such as a hedge fund deciding to take profits. The flip side is that despite daily price fluctuations, crypto can offer a viable refuge for wealth, especially if you reside in a politically unstable area.

PAYMENT FOR LABOR

As an independent contractor, especially in the areas of content creation, information technology, and the analytical consulting businesses, you may wish to get paid via cryptocurrency. By doing so, you avail yourself of all the potential benefits of crypto. However, if you choose this payment option, restrict pay from credible sources only.

As an employer or someone hiring contractors, crypto can be very helpful—especially internationally. After payment, the recipients (employees/contractors) can decide whether to keep their earnings as crypto or to convert them to local currencies. However, if you decide to implement this form of compensation, you should understand the ramifications of the practice for your business. These include the inherent price volatility of some coins, such as

Bitcoin, the need for careful recordkeeping, and the irreversibility of the transactions. Moreover, it's important to instruct those who receive crypto payments from your business to be fully aware of tax consequences.

TIPPING

This is a highly innovative use of crypto based on the Buy Me a Coffee model of digital tipping, but also lets you earn money. You can tip via Brave, a blockchain-based browser that facilitates the process. Additionally, Gitcoin is a crypto platform that allows developers to earn tips for contributing to open-source projects.

Support a Blockchain Platform

As a crypto holder, you can participate in the governance of a blockchain network. Your degree of participation may depend on the amount of currency you own in the platform. That's because the number of votes you can cast depends on the number of coins, or governance tokens, you own. The downside is that it's possible that very large token holders may influence votes in unpopular ways and cause discord inside the platform.

The Dark Side of Anonymity

The potential for risky outcomes with cryptocurrencies is always present. Scams and theft remain a real possibility. To minimize the risk of theft and to avoid becoming a victim of a scam, stick to doing business with liquid coins on credible exchanges with counter parties whom you know and trust.

TYPES OF CRYPTOCURRENCIES

Payment, Exchange Coins, and More

There are multiple types of cryptocurrencies, each with its own set of positive and negative characteristics. Payment cryptos, such as Bitcoin and Ethereum, are the most popular type. Altcoins emerged when independent blockchain programmers made changes to the original Bitcoin code creating Ethereum, which features ether (ETH) (full details on altcoins in Chapter 2). There are also utility tokens that are used to pay for blockchain services, such as apps that can range from gaming to helping you track aspects of your business. Another set of crypto called stablecoins are rapidly growing and are designed to maintain a stable value.

PAYMENT CRYPTOCURRENCIES

Payment cryptocurrencies allow payment transactions to occur. Some popular payment coins include bitcoin (BTC), Bitcoin Cash (BCH), Dogecoin (DOGE), Litecoin (LTC), and Dash (DASH). Payment cryptos must have a set of characteristics to qualify for the category:

- **Portability and acceptability:** They must be widely accepted for payments globally.
- **Divisibility:** They must be portioned (divided into fractions) to pay for items which cost less than a full coin's value.

- **Durability:** A payment crypto must last. Bitcoin, for example, has been successful for years and is widely accepted.
- **Homogeneity:** The coin's value must be universal. Bitcoin A must be equal to Bitcoin B in terms of value.

Without these characteristics, a crypto is not considered a "payment" crypto.

UTILITY TOKENS

Utility tokens (or utility coins) allow access to services on a particular blockchain: keys that let you unlock a particular service like a video game, specific marketplaces, decentralized applications (dApps), or decentralized finance (DeFi) projects. They are mostly used to pay for network fees and to gain access to premium services or content.

Utility tokens are not speculative. Their value is measured in terms of how much accessibility they grant to specific services.

Tokens function on blockchain networks via smart contracts (digital contracts in which the terms of agreement are written directly into code and stored on the blockchain). When predetermined conditions are met, the contract is automatically executed without the need for intermediaries and are efficient and transparent. Execution of smart contracts is irreversible, visible only to the contracted parties, and the code is visible to the entire blockchain. But the ability to interact with the contract is limited to authorized users when conditions are met. These conditions vary, but they require special permissions granted by the blockchain or ownership of the contract (meaning you're a participant in the transaction).

STABLECOINS

Stablecoins are rapidly growing cryptocurrencies. Compared to traditional crypto, the prices of stablecoins fluctuate minimally, rendering them ideal for routine transactions like paying for food delivery or retail shopping. Their stability is due to their being pegged (attached) on a 1:1 basis to the value of a real-world asset, such as the US dollar or gold. For example, if stablecoin A is pegged to the US dollar, the value of the coin will fluctuate along with the dollar.

Popularity Rising for Stablecoins

Stablecoins are increasingly popular as a mainstream payment method. A common use is through gift cards, which can then be used to pay for coffee, fast food, and other traditional retail goods.

EXCHANGE TOKENS

An exchange token is the official exchange method (native cryptocurrency) of a centralized exchange, which mints them as a reward currency for their customers such as reduced trading fees or discounts. The Binance Coin (BNB), for example, pays for goods and services inside and outside of the Binance ecosystem through the Binance Visa card.

MEME COINS

Meme coins are cryptocurrencies based on current Internet memes or trends. They derive their mostly perceived value from the support of the meme's community. Exceptions are Dogecoin (the original meme coin) and Shiba Inu, which have become mainstream cryptos.

Meme coins are created through small changes in the existing code for a prevalent cryptocurrency and often have an unlimited supply. Their price often declines rapidly once the initial hype is over. They can be prone to scams.

GAMEFI CRYPTO

GameFi (game finance) fuses cryptocurrency, decentralized finance, and online gaming into an "in-game economy." The goal is to monetize video games for the players, who are rewarded for their performance via cryptocurrency and other assets/rewards such as digital tokens and in-game prizes like virtual land, avatars, and weapons. The most frequent rewards are non-fungible tokens (NFTs), which can be traded on NFT marketplaces.

SECURITY TOKENS

Security tokens, as the name implies, are securitized versions of crypto assets. So, just like a stock, a security token represents a portion of ownership in a company or the rights to an asset or a company. Generally speaking, a coin is the native cryptocurrency of a specific blockchain while a token is added to the blockchain to function in a specific role within the blockchain. Specifically, security tokens are created via tokenization, a process where an asset's ownership is transferred to a blockchain and converted into a token.

Regulators and taxing authorities view tokens as securities, meaning they can be regulated and taxed. When investing through the blockchain, check if tokens are taxable with an accountant to avoid problems with the Internal Revenue Service (IRS).

NON-FUNGIBLE TOKENS

A non-fungible token (NFT) is part of the blockchain, but it is not a cryptocurrency. Instead, it's a digital representation of a tangible asset, like a painting, that has been tokenized via the blockchain. As with cryptocurrencies, NFTs can be traded by investors via currency, cryptocurrency, or through an exchange for a different NFT. In contrast to actual crypto, such as bitcoins (where one is identical to another), NFTs are all completely unique. Over time, their popularity has decreased, and many are now considered worthless.

PRIVACY COINS

Privacy coins are specialized cryptocurrencies designed to maximize user and transaction anonymity. With these coins, valid concerns about privacy and government influence over finances must be weighed against illicit activity purchased through privacy coins. Both the US and Europe have placed restrictions on this branch of crypto. These coins are a small crypto niche. The following are some of the most common privacy coins.

Monero

This crypto makes transactions difficult to trace via ring signatures and stealth addresses. Ring signatures have blockchain keys assigned to a group of users. These transaction types identify that a member of an authorized group made a transaction, without identifying the individual. A stealth address is like a temporary PO box, a onetime-use crypto wallet address, which can decrease a wallet's ability to be hacked.

Zcash

Zcash is built on a cryptographic method called zero-knowledge proofs, offering two levels of privacy: 1) Allowing transactions between parties without either party being identified, and 2) Hiding the transaction amounts. The level of secrecy involved is limited depending on which side of the transaction one is on. Moreover, the full-privacy features are not triggered by default. Zcash transactions carry higher fees and may face strict regulatory restrictions. Finally, the Zcash platform has lower liquidity than Monero and non-privacy cryptos like Bitcoin.

DASH

Dash offers users the choice of full anonymity and privacy through a protocol titled "CoinJoin," which hides the origin of your funds and charges a higher fee. Dash transactions are nearly instantaneous (similar to credit cards) via its InstantSend feature which can process transactions. Low liquidity may cause problems.

TRADING AND INVESTING IN CRYPTO

The Big Picture

Before diving into the individual currencies, it is important to understand the different strategies one can take when it comes to investing in crypto. As with any financial asset, you can hold cryptocurrencies as a long-term investment, or you can trade them like stocks. So, yes, you can day-trade or trend-trade any crypto by following the basic principles applicable to other asset classes. This entry focuses on the long-term holding approach, but Chapter 6 goes into greater detail and provides many useful strategies and guidelines.

(Note: Since Bitcoin is used as a proxy for the entire crypto system, given that most new coins are derived from it, you should be able to apply this chapter's wisdom to any coin of interest.)

LONG-TERM INVESTING IN CRYPTO

The acronym HODL (Hold On for Dear Life) is derived from a misspelling of the word "hold" in a Bitcoin forum in 2013. The term has been widely accepted by the Bitcoin community, and it defines an investment approach used by long-term holders of the coin. Simply stated, HODLers (or true believers) buy bitcoins and hold them for long periods of time, regardless of the price volatility.

In general, HODLers believe in the notion that cryptocurrencies will eventually replace government-backed currencies. Those holding crypto will be rewarded when others come to use it, making the HODLers' coins rise in value.

Crypto Terminology and Beliefs

There are plenty of other slang terms coined by the crypto community that are now widely used throughout the financial and secular world. Each of the following informs an approach to how crypto investors operate in the financial market:

- **YOLO (You Only Live Once):** This means to put all your money in crypto and let it ride. This state of mind leads to an approach to crypto which is akin to gambling.
- **FOMO (Fear Of Missing Out):** Careful with this one; it refers to emotional investing, often leading to buying crypto just as the market goes south.
- **BTFD (Buy The "Fricking" Dip):** This is the practice of buying into crypto when prices are falling. This is a sensible tactic when properly executed.
- **FUD (Fear, Uncertainty, and Doubt):** This is a term describing indecision, which can lead to making bad decisions both on the buying and selling ends. You can conquer FUD by having a sound approach to crypto.

Each term refers to the behavior of the crypto market and that of an individual or a group. Yet, the simplicity and the pinpoint descriptive accuracy of each make them both humorous and useful. It's important to be able to recognize any market situation to which each term can be applied. Indeed, the most useful of the four, from a trading standpoint, is BTFD.

BTFD requires a sound understanding of how money flows into and out of asset classes and how to recognize them. Capitalizing on this idea involves the understanding of whether a coin is oversold (the sellers are exhausted) and the odds of a meaningful price bottom are in place, thus increasing the odds of success of buying at a low price where there is a solid likelihood of a price advance. There are several useful and reliable techniques to apply this approach in Chapter 6.

HODLING VERSUS TRADING

HODLing is akin to "buy and hold," a strategy used by long-term investors in the stock market. This approach is deployed when you buy crypto systematically, such as on a monthly basis, and hold on to it for years, riding out the price tops and price bottoms.

A refined and often useful method of HODLing is an investment approach known as dollar-cost averaging. For example, let's say you decide to buy $500 worth of crypto monthly. When the price of the coin is high, that $500 may not go very far, but when the price falls, your $500 will buy you more coins, and over time it averages out and you build your holdings at your own pace. The goal is to build a large position in the asset over time, without worrying about whether you're buying at a cheap or an expensive price. The main advantage of this method is that as a HODLer, you'll never miss a rally. The downside is that when the price falls, HODLers watch their paper wealth decrease.

In contrast, when you trade Bitcoin, or any cryptocurrency, you run the risk of being wrong and losing money in the short term. There are several methods of trading cryptocurrencies. Of course, you can use the dollar-cost averaging approach. On the other hand, if you're a more aggressive or risk averse investor, you can apply technical and price chart analysis that may reduce risk. Chapter 6 dives deeply into technically assisted trading methods for crypto.

You may also choose to HODL a portion of your holdings while you trade another portion. This approach lets you hold crypto with some of your assets during down periods, but it also lets you recover a portion of your investment faster when the market turns up.

Ultimately, regardless of the way you approach your investment in crypto, this book offers a viable trading plan and roadmap with the goal of making your investment profitable over time.

To HODL or Not to HODL . . . ?

No matter which approach you take, your best odds of success lie in your full understanding of the approach and your willingness to stick to your investing plan. Perhaps confirm your thoughts with a financial advisor as well.

Chapter 2

Popular Cryptocurrencies

A casual review of a list of cryptocurrencies on an exchange such as Coinbase may show that there are as many as fifty potential investment or trading opportunities in the crypto space. And new coins pop up regularly. However, closer inspection reveals that the list contains representatives from just about any type of crypto that's available, ranging from mainstream trading vehicles like Bitcoin and Ethereum, to stablecoins and even meme coins like Dogecoin.

Regardless of how many different coins are available, there are only two major uses for cryptocurrencies. Some coins are better for one use versus another, while many are excellent vehicles for both. First and foremost, cryptocurrencies are used for investment purposes: both short-term trading and long-term holdings may be part of a diversified portfolio. Second, crypto can be used for transactions, both personal and business. You may use it as a method of payment for goods and services on individual crypto platforms with the platform's native coin as the method of exchange.

As you're getting started, take some time to become familiar with the major coins. Then, as you gain experience and confidence, expand your horizons and explore the niche coins. This chapter focuses on the large, liquid coins that can be used for trading, investment, and transactions, while also mentioning other important coins with large followings and fan bases.

BITCOIN (BTC)

The Original Cryptocurrency

Bitcoin (BTC) is the king of the jungle in the cryptocurrency world. Because so much of crypto is based off of this coin, much of what is said here may apply to other cryptocurrencies as well (unless stated otherwise, of course).

Bitcoin is the most liquid and widely accepted form of crypto, despite some of its limitations. These include its inherent price volatility, struggles with enabling transactions, inherent security risks (like scams and the potential hackability of crypto exchanges), and the lack of insurance compared to other asset classes (like bank deposits). On the other hand, bitcoin certainly serves its intended purpose as an alternative to the traditional government-backed (fiat) payment system. Ultimately, this currency affords its users anonymity while avoiding any government scrutiny of personal transactions.

Crypto Is Legitimate

Crypto as a whole is now widely accepted as both an asset class and a method of exchange. This is confirmed by a June 30, 2025, snapshot of its market valuation of $2.13 trillion sourced from CoinMarketCap.com (https://coinmarketcap.com/currencies/bitcoin), a useful website from which to obtain free general information and current pricing of cryptocurrencies.

AN OVERVIEW OF BITCOIN

Bitcoin was created in 2008 by a mysterious entity/group known as Satoshi Nakamoto, and over time, this currency has become well established and widely accepted. The first bitcoin was mined in 2009 under the name Block 0, also known as the genesis block, signifying this coin's seminal role. Bitcoin began to gain traction in 2010 with the now famous "pizza transaction," where a pizza was purchased for 10,000 BTC. Just one year later, the price of bitcoin reached $1 per coin for the first time.

By 2013, bitcoin reached $1,000 per coin. In 2021, El Salvador became the first country to tag bitcoin as "legal tender." Since then, as of mid-2025, bitcoin's price reached $118,000. These huge numbers are what make it so different from other cryptocurrencies. Bitcoin's appeal spans from day traders to long-term investors, and to anyone who is looking to keep value in a nontraditional way (not using fiat currencies, commodities, or bonds).

However, if you're looking for traditional factors that affect investments like stocks and bonds, such as interest rates, economic data, or earnings reports to affect the price of bitcoin, they don't apply. The truth is that the price of bitcoin (and cryptocurrencies in general) only respond to pure supply and demand.

Simply stated, when there are more buyers than sellers, the price of cryptocurrencies goes up. And when there are more sellers than buyers, the price falls. This dynamic unfolds mostly outside the "normal order" of economic laws or factors that affect the price of stocks, bonds, real estate, gold, or other commodities. In other words, crypto is in its own world and operates under its own rules, which mostly correspond with supply and demand.

FRACTIONING BITCOINS

Because bitcoin is the first coin and it's been around the longest, it's an expensive and volatile asset. If you have a small budget, you likely can't buy full coins to invest. Even if it lost half of its value from a quoted price of $100,000 or more per coin, ownership remains expensive.

This expense issue is solved by the fractioning of bitcoins (splitting the coins into fragments) into satoshis. Each satoshi is worth one-hundred-millionth of a bitcoin. The value of a satoshi is directly related to the price of a bitcoin whenever a transaction is conducted. Satoshis allow Bitcoin holders to make small transactions. Bitcoins and satoshis are fully convertible to other currencies, both crypto and conventional.

Satoshis are expressed mathematically as millibitcoins (mBTC). One mBTC equals 100,000 satoshis. One microbitcoin (µBTC) equals 100 satoshis.

BITCOIN AS A PAYMENT METHOD

In order to use bitcoin to pay for goods or services, the first step is to establish a digital wallet through one of the major crypto exchanges; Binance or Coinbase are the most widely used. Then, you must purchase some bitcoin. Based on your financial condition, you can choose between buying satoshis or entire coins. Then, make transactions by following the generally accepted guidelines on the exchange. You'll find more information on these guidelines in Chapter 4.

The Satoshi Nakamoto Mystery

No discussion of Bitcoin can conclude without asking the question: Who is Satoshi Nakamoto? He is credited with being the creator of Bitcoin, but no one knows who he is. Nakamoto is either a person or a group who created the name and used it as a persona. No one has ever seen Nakamoto, although there are many urban legends about who he might be. We may never know.

Nakamoto has not been heard of since 2011, while speculation is still plentiful as to "his" identity and whereabouts with no apparent end in sight. However, Nakamoto is presumed to be the first Bitcoin miner, and records show that he accumulated 1 million BTC, which at July 2025 price levels would be worth somewhere near $110 trillion.

ETHER (ETH)

The Crypto Opening Up Countless Possibilities

Ether, the native cryptocurrency used on the Ethereum network, is the second most popular cryptocurrency in the world. But don't let its number two ranking understate its presence and potential. While bitcoin is the number one crypto for trading, ether is the number one cryptocurrency for transacting business via smart contracts (digital contracts that are stored on a blockchain and automatically execute specific instructions once the terms of agreement are met, such as ownership transfer of tokens). It also serves as a viable investment method because, like bitcoin and all cryptocurrencies, ether also doubles as a storehouse of value.

ETHEREUM'S HISTORY

Ethereum is a blockchain platform designed for building applications and functions through smart contracts. It was initially proposed in 2013 via a white paper authored by Russian-Canadian computer programmer Vitalik Buterin; one year later, English computer scientist Gavin Wood expanded upon it in his own technical document, the Ethereum Yellow Paper. In 2014, Ethereum, in one of the first initial coin offerings (ICOs), a process similar to an initial public offering (IPO) of stocks where crypto platforms raise capital via the offering of a new coin through sales to the public, raised $18 million. The Ethereum network went live in 2015 with its first incarnation known as "Frontier."

In 2016, the network was hacked, prompting a "hard fork" (an irreversible and major change in a blockchain protocol that splits the network into two blockchains, often creating a new currency). The new blockchain was called Ethereum, which reversed the effects of the hack and refunded the losses to users. It uses the ETH token as its currency. The original currency is housed in a separate blockchain, Ethereum Classic, which uses the ETC token as its currency. Each blockchain operates independently.

In 2017, Ethereum became the leading platform for ICOs. Then came the DeFi summer of 2020, a period when cryptocurrencies and DeFi grew at an alarming rate due to the introduction of new services such as yield farming (collecting interest on crypto holdings) and the advent of lending and borrowing through crypto. These DeFi projects launched on Ethereum. That same year, Ethereum changed from a proof of work (PoW) platform to a proof of stake (PoS) platform. PoW and PoS are transaction validation systems used on crypto platforms. PoW depends on crypto miners solving complex equations to validate transactions, while PoS allows validators to confirm transactions based on the number of coins they have staked. PoS is more energy efficient and can lead to faster transaction processing, which has helped Ethereum gain in popularity. You can find more details in the "How Ethereum Works" section later in this entry. As of 2025, Ethereum celebrated its tenth year of existence.

THE UNIQUENESS OF ETHEREUM

In reality, the differences between the terms "Ethereum" and "ether" (ETH) have been blurred by familiarity. Technically speaking, Ethereum is a software platform, while ether is the coin that fuels transactions on the platform. So, where Bitcoin is primarily a trading and investment asset, Ethereum is intended to be a self-contained world. Ethereum's goal is to be a central cog in the emerging Internet known as Web3.

Ethereum functions through smart contracts (digital contracts in which the terms of the agreement are coded directly onto the blockchain) and decentralized operations (alternatives to current corporate and financial structures). Smart contracts formalize an agreement between two parties and preserve it through blockchain code. The agreement involves key components as to what the conditions of the contract will be and how it will be executed, including rules of conduct and consequences for breaches of the contract. Once the smart contract is finished, it's deployed onto the blockchain and it's irreversible. Smart contracts have many possible uses; you can employ them to design a savings plan, determine estate planning, and even to define and trigger an insurance contract in response to a natural disaster.

HOW ETHEREUM WORKS

To accomplish its goals, Ethereum uses executable code in its blockchain structure, which is how it has transitioned beyond a transaction recording mechanism, such as Bitcoin. Ethereum uses proof of stake (PoS) as a validation mechanism, as opposed to proof of work (PoW), which is the basis for Bitcoin transactions. PoS requires validators (participants in the networks who act as gatekeepers), to put up their tokens to validate transactions, while

PoW is a complex puzzle-solving mechanism that pits competing computers against one another in order to complete transactions.

PoS is considered more environmentally friendly than PoW because it involves fewer participants and decongests the network, thus reducing energy usage. PoW is a competitive process that attracts large numbers of participants. PoS is seen as less risky to the status of the network, since any validators have to prove they are stakeholders to participate. Many new coins are now adopting the PoS protocol.

DIFFERENCES BETWEEN BITCOIN AND ETHEREUM

There are some key distinctions between Bitcoin and Ethereum. Unlike Bitcoin, which has a 21 million coin issuance limit, Ethereum has no limits, meaning a coin's value can suffer periods of stagnation as the number of coins increases. This is a perfect example of one aspect of supply and demand. Additionally, Ethereum transactions take as little as 12 seconds, while Bitcoin transactions can take 10 minutes or longer; this makes Ethereum more attractive as a transactional method for many. Finally, the odds of a transaction being cancelled via Ethereum are much lower than with Bitcoin, easing the total potential bottlenecks in the system.

ETHEREUM'S FUTURE

Ethereum's flexibility as a platform is expanding. Some unique uses of this currency include the use of Ethereum-based tokens to distribute royalties in the music business and its emerging role for innovation in the crypto and blockchain universes.

Ultimately, Bitcoin and Ethereum are different versions of crypto. Each has evolved in distinct ways, but both are considered reasonable methods of conducting financial transactions. Bitcoin is primarily an investment vehicle, both in terms of its use for speculation (trading) and long-term investing (HODLing). However, Ethereum is rapidly evolving due to its user-friendly and practical, smart contract–based platform architecture. It's both a financial asset and a diversified financial universe through which decentralized financing and applications are expanding. There's plenty of room for both coins, although Ethereum has the potential to grow at a faster pace.

Hacking Ethereum

It is theoretically possible that a hack of the Ethereum system could occur if a single validator was to hold 51% of all the ether coins. The odds of that are almost nil due to the market capitalization of the coin ($470 billion as of November 2025).

ADA (CARDANO)

Yet Another Evolutionary Trail

Cardano is a blockchain platform with its own coin named ADA. Much of this coin's architecture is built on what seems to work for other large coins, such as bitcoin and ether. Despite some controversies, this coin has made a name for itself in the crypto coin market.

CARDANO'S HISTORY

Cardano was started by Charles Hoskinson, a cofounder of Ethereum, who left the Ethereum platform in 2014 after disagreements related to the direction of Ethereum. Hoskinson started the development of Cardano one year later, and the first block was mined in 2017. Thus, it should not be surprising that Cardano defines itself as an alternative to Ethereum, billing itself as a "third generation" platform, while describing Ethereum as a "second generation" platform. Its stated goal is to provide banking services to the "unbanked" (meaning, those who do not use banks in any capacity).

Cardano's history is a study in complexity, where the system continues to evolve to a higher level of function with each subsequent change. In 2016, the Cardano Foundation was formed to promote the use of the Cardano coin (ADA). The coin's development was originally conducted by the software engineering corporation Input Output Hong Kong, now known as Input Output Global.

ABOUT CARDANO

On its own, Cardano is a middling cryptocurrency and ADA is somewhat of a niche coin with a large enough market cap ($23 billion as of November 2025) to be considered a major player, a factor that is reinforced by a large and enthusiastic following. However, since its price in November 2025 was below $1, it is not considered a true money magnet like bitcoin and ether. As with many next generation coins, it's designed to be the next generation ether-based coin, offering its users many of the same potential benefits and uses as ether if they transact on the Cardano platform.

Daedalus and Nodes

Cardano has its own cryptocurrency wallet known as Daedalus, which boasts the capacity to run a full "node" on every device it's installed on. A node is a computer or server that is connected to a blockchain network. Their function is to store and ensure the continuity and decentralized structure of the blockchain. Think of nodes as backup sites for the entire blockchain, decreasing the odds of a major malfunction interfering with the operation of the chain. Nodes can perform specific functions including validation of transactions, mining, serving as data archives, and security functions.

Eco-Friendly

Aside from being the banker for the "unbanked," Cardano wants to be the most environmentally sustainable crypto platform through its PoS protocol called Ouroboros, which uses less energy to operate than Bitcoin. The Cardano blockchain is divided into two separate layers, the Cardano Settlement Layer (CSL) and the Cardano Computing Layer (CCL). The CSL is the recordkeeping branch (and where the transactions are validated via Ouroboros), and CCL is where all the operations, such as smart contracts and decentralized operations, are conducted. By splitting the platform into two separate branches, it can transact a larger number of transactions more efficiently, which improves its energy usage and helps it to work toward its sustainability goal.

Ouroboros Global Maintenance

The Ouroboros system is verified and maintained by computer scientists and cryptographers from major global universities, such as the University of Tokyo. It's the first system of its kind and is considered a major step to increase the security of a blockchain. It's also considered environmentally friendly.

Cardano also offers some flexibility if you're a programmer, as you can create native tokens on the platform without using smart contracts, although the platform is based on Ethereum-like smart contract technology. This ability to create native tokens without smart contracts is supposed to make the tokens more secure and to lower transaction fees. Cardano hopes to be governed by its stakeholders in the future with a system similar to that of proxy votes for major corporations, meaning that the more tokens you hold, the more you can influence the way the platform works.

HOW CARDANO STANDS OUT

Although Cardano shares the basic characteristics of all cryptocurrencies, it clearly stands out from the others. An interesting aspect of its history is its constant evolution through hard forks, which have spawned multiple "eras" in the platform's history. Each era has its own name, which began with Byron and evolved into Shelley, Allegra, Mary, Alonzo, Lobster, Vasil, Valentine, Chang, and Plomin (as of January 2025). Each hard fork added a new layer of functionality to the chain, with the Plomin fork putting all the previous forks together while expanding on the platform's governance.

What differentiates Cardano from Bitcoin is its inherent design to be a universal tool available to all users, especially programmers, while streamlining many processes (including mining) and its implementation of smart contracts. As a result, it's a community project; it will likely continue to evolve as it encounters hard forks. In its current expression, Cardano is attractive due to its efficiency as a transactional mechanism, while Ethereum and Bitcoin remain attractive trading vehicles.

SOLANA (SOL)

The Jackrabbit of the Crypto World

Solana is a cryptocurrency that runs on the Solana platform and is designed for decentralized and scalable operations. As with many other cryptocurrencies, Solana was created to improve specific aspects of the ecosystem. Specifically, its entry into the world of cryptocurrencies was designed to address energy usage and transactional speed. Since its introduction, Solana has gained a strong following. This entry walks through the crypto's history, its many efficiencies, how it compares to other cryptos, and how to use Solana. Though intricate, this mid-sized crypto is definitely worth the watch.

SOLANA'S HISTORY

Solana was founded in 2017 by Anatoly Yakovenko and Raj Gokal. It's an open-source project run by the Solana Foundation in Zug, Switzerland. The original blockchain was built in San Francisco by Solana Labs. The platform was launched in 2020.

Though it's newer than the cryptocurrencies discussed so far, the founders certainly have their credentials. Yakovenko has experience programming for tech giants like Qualcomm. He realized that software with a built-in clock is more efficient, improving the synchronization and efficiency of networks. Thus, he built Solana as a PoS blockchain that incorporates a clock. Meanwhile, Gokal is a behind-the-scenes player, running the business side of Solana. He has experience as a financial analyst, with a focus on investment banking, and has worked on Wall Street.

SOLANA VERSUS OTHER CRYPTOS

Solana can process transactions much faster than Ethereum with lower transaction fees, while benefitting from being a well-run business entity. Like Ethereum, Solana is a proof of stake (PoS) blockchain, and it's enhanced by the proof of history (PoH) protocol, which is based on a clock to timestamp transactions. It's similar to Ethereum because of its use of PoS and smart contracts.

By adding the clock element, the transaction time speeds up drastically—Solana can process over 2,400 transactions per second. This is a pace more closely aligned with traditional payment protocols such as Visa, whose rate is 65,000 transactions per second. Meanwhile, Bitcoin and Ethereum process up to 15 transactions per second. The PoH protocol verifies the amount of time between events and records them on a ledger.

Moreover, Solana is designed to remove bottlenecks in the blockchain with insiders projecting that the system may be able to process 710,000 transactions per second at some point in the future.

A Broad Comparison of Solana and Ethereum

Ethereum has the advantage of having been the first cryptocurrency to expand beyond Bitcoin's design. Yet, Solana's refinements of the Ethereum blockchain model have made it a serious player. So, while both Solana and Ethereum use smart contracts and the PoS protocol, Solana also uses PoH, which offers a diversified, more secure platform. Additionally, the transaction speed has made Solana popular with gamers and non-fungible token (NFT) platforms. Aside from its faster processing fees, Solana also has lower fees than Ethereum ($0.00026 versus $0.30 per transaction as of July 2025). Moreover, Ethereum fees can be highly variable depending on network congestion, which Ethereum names gas fees, a rate structure that measures the number of resources used by validators in order to calculate their rewards.

SOLANA WALLET COMPARISONS

Solana users can trade, lend, and borrow assets. Before you start, you must establish a wallet via exchanges such as Coinbase or the Phantom wallet. Phantom is designed especially to be used with Solana (though it supports others like Ethereum and Bitcoin).

Although the Phantom wallet caters mostly to Solana, it boasts a user-friendly interface to conduct transactions, especially the trading of Solana-supported tokens through its built-in swap system, which allows users to switch between Solana's native coin (SOL) and other tokens. You can also conduct your swaps through platforms such as MoonPay. The process involves connecting your wallet to MoonPay and following the directions (www.moonpay .com/swap/sol). This feature is especially attractive to Solana-focused users who want to avoid simplifying their conversions from between tokens, as multiple accounts won't be required to trade between different types of tokens (including NFTs). The Phantom wallet is available through a web browser and a mobile app. Unfortunately, as with any crypto platform, Phantom wallets have been exposed to fraud, with some wallets being "drained" of all their funds via scams and hacks. Though rare, these things happen. MoonPay has no history of being directly hacked, but there have been instances of successful phishing attacks on its executives (for example, in June 2025). The attacks resulted in the transfer of $250,000 in stablecoins by the phished executives to a fraudulent wallet. It's not clear whose funds were transferred or whether they've been recovered as of November 2025.

To reduce the risk of being hacked, Solana users can also use a Ledger wallet. This is a physical device, similar to an external USB drive, that works like a minicomputer and offers the same type of transactional convenience and adaptability as virtual wallets such as Coinbase and Phantom. However, once you disconnect the Ledger from the online world, you're basically holding your crypto in a physical vault. Additionally, Ledger wallets are protected by high level security when you're connected. You can use Ledger wallets with any cryptocurrency.

THE SOLANA PLAYGROUND

An interesting aspect of Solana's operations is the Solana Playground, an online tool that allows programmers to design and test programs to later deploy on the platform. It requires the creation of a Playground wallet, which in turn requires a wallet address (a public key to the platform, acting similarly to an email address). Further steps are required before you can develop and deploy programs on the network, but this user-friendly approach encourages participation in the platform and is an important part of Solana's appeal.

Solana's Future

Solana continues to attract followers, yet as with many cryptocurrencies, its future is uncertain due to the evolving landscape and the market dominance of Bitcoin, Ethereum, XRP Ledger, and Binance. But with its focus on interaction with its users, Solana has a steadily growing appeal and following.

XRP

Ripple's Native Coin

The cryptocurrency XRP is multifaceted, as it's used for both transactions and trading. It's rather complicated, as it's used by businesses and financial institutions for global transactions, although XRP is available to anyone. It's the native token of XRP Ledger, an open-source blockchain.

Defining a Native Token

Native tokens are the primary cryptocurrencies designed to facilitate transactions and paying fees on any blockchain platform. Each blockchain has its own native token, which is directly built into the platform and is essential for trading, lending, transaction validation, and even network security. Native tokens are created on the platform internally, while non-native tokens are created on top of the blockchain, often through the creation of smart contracts. A salient example of a non-native token is wrapped bitcoin (WBTC), which is a tokenized version of bitcoin operating on the Ethereum platform.

XRP'S HISTORY

XRP was created in 2011 and launched in 2012 by David Schwartz, Jed McCaleb, and Arthur Britto. Schwartz was the chief technical officer of Ripple, a company associated with XRP, until recently. He stepped down as of October 1, 2025. Schwartz is an expert cryptographer who used to work for the National Security Agency

(NSA). McCaleb is a tech sector entrepreneur and an expert programmer. Britto stays primarily behind the scenes, but there are whispers that he's the backbone of the operation.

The original project was named Ripple, which included XRP (the token), the Ripple Consensus Ledger, the Ripple Transaction Protocol, and the Ripple Network. The OpenCoin company was a co-developer of the XRP Ledger and was renamed Ripple Labs (now just Ripple). The XRP Ledger Foundation was formed in 2020 and functions to maintain and further develop the XRP Ledger (a blockchain), where XRP operates.

ABOUT XRP

As with other platforms, the XRP cryptocurrency and blockchain aim to improve transactional efficiency, especially involving financial transfers and exchanging one cryptocurrency for another. This is especially targeting transactions between large financial corporations. Investors also use it to store value and profit from price fluctuations. In terms of its ranking, XRP's market cap in July 2025 was in the range of $8 billion.

XRP is often used by financial institutions. It's accessed through the blockchain services company, Ripple, for cross-border transfers and currency exchanges. Ripple and XRP are totally independent from one another, though Ripple uses the XRP platform for transactions due to its simplicity.

XRP is widely used and offers users access to XRP-based derivative investments, such as futures and options. There are no traditional fees for using transactions with XRP. Instead, a portion of a coin, equal to a fee amount, is "burned" (removed from the platform) with each transaction. So, burning is really just a fee charged by Ripple on XRP transactions.

XRP operates via the XRP Ledger (XRPL), which is the blockchain for the platform; XRPL keeps records of transactions that use XRP (the token). The distinguishing feature between XRP and other coins is that, by design, it's targeted for use by businesses. Similar to Bitcoin, XRP has a limited supply of tokens (100 billion). Moreover, XRP is pre-mined, a process through which the coins are created for a group of insiders (such as investors or creators) before they are offered to the public via an initial coin offering (ICO).

Pre-Mining Controversies

Interestingly, pre-mining is a somewhat controversial topic. The practice is seen as favoring a certain group of insiders instead of the entire community. The purpose of pre-mining, according to its proponents, is to fund the system via early investment, raise awareness of an upcoming release of the coin, and pay contractors for development work. It's not unheard of, as a significant portion of the total supply of ether coins was pre-mined, while 50 BTC were pre-mined prior to their ICO.

Other Controversies

Pre-mining is not the only controversy tied to Ripple and XRP. In December 2020, the US Securities and Exchange Commission (SEC) accused Ripple of selling unregistered securities via XRP. In 2023, a court ruling imposed penalties against Ripple, which included a $125 million fine. Although Ripple appealed, they eventually withdrew it and, after a nearly five-year legal battle, the case ended in August 2025, with Ripple paying the $125 million to the

US Treasury. The outcome sets a legal precedence that will likely affect the regulation of and the activities of crypto companies.

The bottom line is that XRP is an interesting cryptocurrency that has the potential to influence how large institutions transfer money around the world. The resolution of the SEC-related legal issues will have a profound effect on the crypto universe.

BINANCE COIN (BNB)

The Native Coin of the Largest Crypto Exchange

Binance is the birthplace of one of the leading cryptocurrencies, Binance Coin (BNB). Binance Coin is a highly successful enterprise but has also experienced some troubled times due to what some global authorities have described as "lax" adherence to regulations. Through all of its controversies, Binance has proven its resiliency, having become the largest decentralized exchange, which is similar in function to a stock exchange but distinctly different because, in the spirit of crypto's independence from traditional finance, a decentralized exchange does not include middlemen such as banks.

BINANCE'S HISTORY

Founded in China in 2017, Binance initially moved to Japan to avoid Chinese regulatory requirements, then relocated once more to Malta. Its rapid growth has spawned a global presence with an additional office in Singapore and other locations, where the company lists its headquarters. Its coin, Binance Coin, was founded in 2017.

Binance cofounder Changpeng Zhao pleaded guilty to a money laundering charge in November 2023 and was sentenced to four months in prison in April 2024, along with a $50 million fine. Binance was fined $4.3 billion. Zhao was released in September of that same year. The case was built around allegations that Binance was allowing criminals to use its platform for illicit activities such as human and narcotics trafficking. After the settlement and Zhao's exit, Binance's reputation recovered and it continued its growth and development. As of August 2025, Binance services over 280 million users. Changpeng Zhao was pardoned by President Trump in October 2025.

ABOUT BINANCE

Binance supports trading and related services in over five hundred cryptocurrencies, including bitcoin and ether. Through Binance, users can make spot, margin, or futures trades; plus, the company offers low fees, a user-friendly platform, direct (peer-to-peer) trading opportunities between parties, and a mobile app. Binance also offers opportunities for rewards through staking, where users agree not to trade or sell their tokens in order to keep the blockchain running smoothly. Users receive rewards for staking. Users also earn interest on crypto holdings through the Binance Earn program, which allows for staking as well as yield farming where users receive rewards for lending their crypto to other users in exchange for interest (a process similar to traditional loans). For beginners, Binance offers a wide variety of educational information in the form of tutorials and easy-to-digest guides. Through Binance, crypto users can buy, sell, and store their cryptocurrencies; this includes bitcoin, ether, Binance Coin, and others. In July 2025, Binance housed over $160 billion in digital assets.

Binance Coin (BNB) is its native coin/token through which business is conducted on the exchange. BNB is used to pay for transactions on the Binance blockchain and as a utility token that lets users pay for transaction fees and lets them participate in the network's mechanism for creating consensus. It's built on Ethereum's blockchain and has a strict maximum of 200 million BNB tokens in circulation. The company buys and retires (burns) coins held in its treasury to maintain the limit.

Binance was first released as an ERC-20 token on the Ethereum blockchain but has since migrated to its own blockchain, the Binance Chain, which has two sections: the BNB Beacon Chain (recordkeeping and governance) and the BNB Smart Chain (handling smart contracts and transactions). Binance offers the following discounts and advantages to its users:

- 25% on spot trading fees
- 25% on margin trading fees
- 10% on futures trading fees
- The ability to conduct token sales
- Staking rewards that don't require large numbers of coins to participate
- Ease of use for other platforms

Additionally, Binance operates by the proof of stake (PoS) mechanism, where validators confirm transactions and create new blocks; it is also combined with proof of authority (PoA). PoA is a mechanism that uses "known and reputable" validators to produce blocks on the chain. PoA is designed for corporate entities who wish to develop their own closed blockchains. Moreover, the combined fee structure offered by Binance (discounts, VIP levels, and referral cashback programs) increase the platform's low-cost structure. The combination of PoA and PoS enhances platform security, and reduces block time and transaction fees while increasing network efficiency.

THE BINANCE VIP PROGRAM

The Binance VIP Program offers "high-volume digital asset traders" lower trading fees depending on which program tier they fit into; the program tier is based on how much you trade. The VIP program offers lower fees and access to the VIP portal, a specialized trading platform designed to deliver a more streamlined trading environment. In addition, it's scalable, meaning you can be bumped up to the next VIP level by increasing your trading volume (levels 1–9 are available).

The VIP platform isn't cheap; it requires a thirty-day average asset holding/trading volume of at least $250,000 to $1,000,000 to qualify for the upper tiers. The bare minimum to qualify is some combination of $100,000 of borrowing or holding 25 BNB coins. But here's the kicker: If you're a VIP on another platform, you can switch to Binance through its VIP Invitation Program. The VIP Program rewards users who are willing to take on higher trading risks via larger trading volume and higher use of margin to execute trades.

Ultimately, what sets Binance apart from other cryptocurrencies is its operation: The BNB Smart Chain is a blockchain that offers lower fees and faster transaction speeds compared to other blockchains (such as Ethereum) thanks to its combined use of PoS and PoA mechanisms. Moreover, the Binance Coin is highly liquid, meaning it can be converted into another digital asset without significantly affecting its price. Finally, Binance is an important cog in the cryptocurrency universe, much of it due to its association with the Binance exchange and related ecosystem components.

The Binance Coin's Many Uses

The most common uses of the Binance Coin are for payment for transaction fees on the Binance blockchain, travel bookings (accepted at TravelbyBit and others), entertainment (buying music and game rewards), online services (Canva and others), and financial services such as taking out a loan at Aave or to invest in ICOs offered through Binance.

TRONIX (TRX), TONCOIN (TON), AND ALGO

Three PoS Small Coins with High Potential

As the crypto universe continues to grow, some coins have a low market cap. But, as history shows, these market caps do not equate to a coin's insignificance. The likelihood that today's meme could be tomorrow's bitcoin shouldn't be discounted. This entry focuses on lower priced cryptocurrencies with excellent future potential because of some of the inherent properties they bring into the mix and their appeal to individual groups of users.

TRONIX (TRX)

Tronix (TRX) is the native coin that is used to make transactions on the Tron platform, which is based on the Ethereum platform and runs on a PoS mechanism. Created in 2017 by originally Beijing-based entrepreneur Justin Sun (whose whereabouts are uncertain, with some reports suggesting he lives in Hong Kong while others say he now resides in Florida, US). Tron is a late arrival in the crypto universe.

Tron runs on a delegated PoS consensus mechanism, where system users vote for Super Representatives (SRs) whose job is to validate transactions, produce blocks, and maintain network security. To become SRs, users apply and pay a fee of 9,999 TRX. Then, if accepted, SRs gain voting rights by staking TRX tokens.

Each staked token gives the SR one vote. This is known as Tron Power. SRs have a governing role in the community with the top twenty-seven candidates (measured by the number of votes received) gaining governance power. SRs ranked 27–128 receive rewards but not voting rights. Rewards include 16 TRX tokens for every block produced. Votes, which determine protocol upgrades and network parameters, are counted every 6 hours. Only the latest count by an SR is recorded.

TRX has a low value, with the November 2, 2025, quote being $0.2964 versus the US dollar as listed on CoinMarketCap.com (https://coinmarketcap.com/currencies/tron/). On that same day, Bitcoin traded near $110,000. That said, Tron is a platform worth keeping an eye on, as it's become a central cog in the stablecoin segment of crypto. Tron was created to decentralize the content creation industry and features multiple tokens: BitTorrent (BTT), JUST (JST), and a version of the Tether stablecoin. What separates Tron from other platforms, however, is that content on the Tron platform can be accessed by anyone with an Internet connection, thus bypassing censorship hurdles.

TONCOIN (TON)

Toncoin is the native currency of a blockchain network called The Open Network. Its market cap in August 2025 was in the vicinity of $8 billion. Toncoin is an open-sourced coin that allows for many contributors, including a Swiss nonprofit called the TON Foundation. TON has been developed by independent contributors and enthusiasts of the platform. Though TON was originally linked with controversial European social media giant Telegram until 2020, the SEC ordered Telegram to end its affiliation with TON. So, at least on paper, Telegram has nothing to do with TON, although TON is still used widely on Telegram.

That said, TON has its merits and it's certainly ambitious in design. It is a Layer-1 blockchain, as are Bitcoin, Ethereum, Solana, and Cardano. Layer-1 blockchains are designed to be built upon, or to become the founding blockchains of other coins and serve as the backbone for decentralized apps (dAPPs) used on the network and related platforms. TON is used for trading, transactions, fee collection, dApps, and other services on the TON platform.

TON is particularly attractive to developers of games inside the TON network, as the coin serves as a method of rewarding game participants and powering the games' economic transactions. Additionally, outside of this, some merchants and service providers offer discounts and special perks for using TON for their products and services. If you have a business and wish to take TON as a payment method, you can set up a payment system through Binance by creating an account, signing an agreement, and integrating access to the Binance Pay app into your website.

ALGO

ALGO is the native coin of Algorand, a PoS blockchain that is seen as a major advancement in the crypto universe. The platform was developed in 2017 by MIT professor Silvio Micali and launched in 2019. Interestingly, in addition to its technology appeal, the platform has developed interesting partnerships, including arrangements with Italy's largest olive oil producers and World Chess. Algorand bills itself as a platform built to challenge the status quo by addressing the so-called "blockchain trilemma": security, scalability, and decentralization.

By crypto standards, Algorand is a small fish in a big pond. In August 2025, its market cap was $2.26 billion and its trading price in US dollars was $0.26. Its all-time high price of $2.82 was reached in 2021.

What Sets Algorand Apart

Algorand's PPoS (Pure Proof-of-Stake) protocol contains validators that are randomly chosen but not required to lock up their staked tokens. So, where traditional PoS chooses validators based on the amount of cryptocurrency they hold, PPoS evens the playing field by its randomizing of the choice of validators. This increases the speed of transactions while not negatively impacting security. This process reduces the concentration of transaction validations by the largest stakeholders in the platform, thus evening out the playing field by not letting those with the most tokens rule the platform, while reducing transaction speed. Transactions can occur in 3 seconds and Algorand's protocol can perform as many as 10,000 transactions per second. The PPoS protocol is ultimately considered to be very user-friendly, while its security system, named Byzantine, is highly efficient. In addition, Algorand is considered a carbon-neutral blockchain.

Algorand can be utilized in many cool ways. For example, with Lofty (a real estate marketplace) investors can invest in real estate through ALGO for as little as $50, then quickly cash in without major paperwork. Another example is with the ALGO-based Folks Finance platform, where users can trade, stake, lend, and borrow money, receiving lower fees than traditional financial institutions. Plus, an underappreciated advantage of Folks Finance is its scalability; over time, this feature will help keep fees from rising too rapidly as demand picks up.

Other Algorand Investing Opportunities

Algorand users can invest in precious metals through Meld Gold, where 1 token buys 1 gram of gold or silver. Humanitarian organizations can expand their donor base via the HesabPay platform. Stablecoin fans can use the ALGO-based Quantoz Payments stablecoin, which is a fully regulated euro-based coin that allows users to make payments in euros with less hassle than through traditional methods.

CENTRAL BANK DIGITAL CURRENCIES (CBDC)

Governments Joining the Digital Currency Phenomenon

It's no surprise that a new digital currency has attracted the attention of global governments, especially that of central banks. The US Federal Reserve defines a central bank digital currency (CBDC) as a "digital form of central bank money that is widely available to the general public." However, their presence in the world is as uniquely complex as the many forms of cryptocurrencies available.

ABOUT CBDCS

Central bank digital currencies threaten to take away the most attractive aspect of cryptocurrency: anonymity. Once central banks get involved, the government's involved, which means surveillance. Of course, if the government truly wants to investigate crypto transactions, it can do so anytime—with or without CBDCs.

Speaking of Governmental Power

In early June 2025, the US Department of Justice announced it had confiscated more than $225 million in cryptocurrency. The Secret Service, the US Attorney's Office, and the Federal Bureau of Investigation (FBI) combined to investigate thousands of blockchain transactions until they isolated the wallets involved in a global crypto-based scam and money laundering scheme.

CBDCs are part of the digital currency universe, already well embedded into the financial landscape in parts of the world. However, there is a positive side to CBDCs: They are perfect replicas of a country's fiat currencies and are thus backed by that country's legal tender promise. This means you can use these currencies in the same way, for the same purposes that you use paper money or coins.

Interestingly, in contrast to the viewpoint of those who oppose CBDCs, the Federal Reserve notes that its goal is not to replace paper cash with a digital currency, but to provide an alternative way to use the US dollar. Indeed, the Fed is currently in the process of seeking public comments before deciding whether to proceed with a CBDC. Moreover, among the pros and cons of a US CBDC, the Fed acknowledges that it must strike a "balance" when it comes to transactional privacy, if and when the digital dollar is deployed.

TYPES OF CBDCS

There are two types of central bank digital currencies: wholesale and retail. The former is designed to be used by institutions (like banks and financial services companies) and should function similarly to official reserves held in a central bank. These accounts allow banks to deposit funds directly into the central bank; they're also used to conduct monetary policy by the central bank. For example, they may buy and sell bonds to lower or raise interest rates or to control money supply.

Retail CBDCs are used by businesses and consumers to conduct business as with tangible, paper cash and are accessible via private keys, public keys, or both. A private key is like an ID; it is an access code issued in a 64-digit hexadecimal format that is generated by a crypto wallet, representing your ownership of the cryptocurrency. A public key, on the other hand, is a hashed version of a private key and creates a crypto address, most often used as a signature.

More Information on Private and Public Keys

When you make a crypto transaction, you receive a private and a public key. The private key is issued to the owner, authorizing the transaction. The public key proves ownership of the private key and creates public addresses. Although a public key is created from a private key, it is nearly impossible to create a private key from a public key.

COUNTRIES WHERE CBDCS ARE ACTIVE

Jamaica, The Bahamas, and Nigeria have fully deployed CBDCs. Yet, there is resistance within these populations, and they are not fully integrated into their financial systems. The most advanced CBDC-using country is China, where the digital yuan (e-CNY) can be used in transportation systems, e-commerce networks, and payroll distribution networks. It's not anonymous; the government knows exactly what each digital yuan is doing with the push of a button. According to the government, this lack of anonymity is by design; this way, people don't attempt tax evasion. The European Union, through its own central bank, is studying the potential for a digital euro. In contrast to China's approach, one of its main focuses is privacy.

SECURITY AND UTILITY TOKENS

Variations of Cryptos

Security and utility tokens are important variations of cryptocurrencies. Specifically, security tokens represent ownership of a portion of an entity. Utility tokens, on the other hand, offer access to specific services on a blockchain. Moreover, security tokens are regulated while most utility tokens are not. Reminder: A token is a long string of numbers and letters, and the transfer of ownership of an asset to a blockchain is known as tokenization. By combining the two processes, you arrive at the creation of both utility and security tokens.

COMPARING THE TOKENS AND CRYPTO

Security tokens, utility tokens, and cryptocurrencies are all blockchain-related assets. However, it's important to understand the differences between them. While cryptocurrencies are designed to be an exchange mechanism, security and utility tokens are designed to provide proof of ownership.

To break it down, tokenization offers access to goods and services on any given blockchain. So, a security token that's based on shares (ownership) of a publicly traded company is a tokenized version of shares held with a licensed custodian (a regulated financial entity that functions to house and safeguard crypto assets). Additionally, a utility token offers access to goods and services on a blockchain platform.

Here's a summary of the nuts and bolts of the "securitization" of a token:

- A company defines what the token represents and transfers the information to a blockchain.
- The company offers the token to investors.
- Ownership of the token is recorded on the blockchain.
- Tokens can then be held, used, or traded by the investors.

Security tokens and cryptocurrencies are nearly identical *except* for the way they are used. Cryptocurrencies are used like conventional currencies, and security tokens are used in a similar way to stock certificates, as they are the official proof of ownership, just as a stock certificate would proof your ownership of 100 shares of Nvidia.

Here's a great way to illustrate the difference between the two types of tokens. Binance Coin (BNB) is the utility token of the Binance ecosystem and is used for paying for services on the Binance blockchain platform. On the other hand, bNVDA is a security token through which, as detailed in the next section, shares of semiconductor giant Nvidia are traded on the Ethereum blockchain for non-US users.

Security Tokens

An advantage of security tokens is the ability to trade company shares all the time, even when native markets are closed. Plus, users have self-custody of the assets, as they are held in their crypto wallets. Additionally, security tokens can be used as collateral in blockchain transactions. Finally, all payments and other transactions related to the security token are funded and conducted in crypto.

One example of a security token is the Backed Nvidia (bNVDA) token. This is a tokenized version of the shares of the semiconductor company Nvidia, which is available to non-US investors. It's a tokenized certificate of ownership of shares in the company, and its price tracks the price of the shares. This token is designed to combine the benefits of blockchain technology and the real world by offering investors the opportunity to own shares in the company via a blockchain platform.

Another interesting example of a security token is a tokenized certificate of the iShares Core S&P 500 ETF, which offers 1:1 ownership of shares in the ETF to non-US citizens. The tokens are backed by ETF shares held by third-party Swiss custodians. This product allows simple access to the US stock market to international investors via a simplified method that does not require opening a US brokerage account.

Utility Tokens

Utility tokens are crypto tokens designed to allow users access to specific products or services within specified blockchains. Unlike security tokens, utility tokens do not represent ownership of property or assets. They are also less tightly regulated. Here's a list of popular utility tokens outside of the Bitcoin, Ethereum, and Solana platforms:

- **Chainlink (LINK):** LINK is the utility token for the Chainlink platform, which connects smart contracts to real-time data. Use LINK to pay for platform services such as financial news feeds, weather information, or sports scores.
- **Filecoin (FIL):** This utility token is the key to the Filecoin decentralized storage platform. Use FIL to pay for storage space or to receive payments for renting out storage space.

- **The Sandbox (SAND):** Use SAND to monetize or pay for virtual content in the Sandbox metaverse.
- **Basic Attention Token (BAT):** The Basic Attention Token is used for rewarding users and advertisers on the Brave browser, a privacy-focused browser that blocks trackers and ads.

There are pros and cons to utility tokens. The pros are that these tokens offer conveniency and privacy when interacting on a blockchain platform, while offering the platform the ability to raise capital without offering equity. The cons are best summed up in the context of the platform itself and how much traction it gains. As expected, the more popular the platform, the greater the value of the token.

Rules and Regulations for Utility Tokens

The regulatory framework for utility tokens varies internationally. In the US, some of these tokens are seen as traditional securities and are regulated by the SEC. Always check the regulatory environment before putting your money down.

Chapter 3

Stablecoins

Imagine a scenario in which a merchant sells a bedroom furniture suite to a customer for $5,000 worth of bitcoin. When the merchant tries to convert that bitcoin to fiat dollars, she discovers the bitcoin stake is now only worth $1,000. This is an unfortunate reality, and the cryptocurrency system needed a dose of price stability. Stablecoins are crypto's answer to the price volatility, which is inherent to bitcoin, ether, and the rest of the tradeable coins.

Stablecoins are designed to keep crypto values within narrow ranges so that they can be used for just about any transaction. These can range from the mundane, such as grocery shopping, to the more intense reality, such as buying cars and homes, with predictable outcomes.

Unlike traded cryptocurrency coins with value based only on supply and demand, a stablecoin's value is pegged to a tangible asset. These may vary from a major currency (the dollar or the euro), a commodity (gold), a financial instrument (another cryptocurrency), or as confusing as it seems, an algorithm (a set of computer rules designed to keep the value of the coin stable). In other words, stablecoins are a promise by the crypto world to hold the value of cryptocurrencies stable. This and more are covered in further detail throughout this chapter, which explains how stablecoins work and explores the various stablecoins available.

THE BASIC TENETS OF STABLECOINS

Dampening Volatility in the Crypto World

Stablecoins are cryptocurrencies designed to maintain a stable price by "pegging" their price to a separate asset. A peg links the price of an asset to a separate asset. When a stablecoin is pegged to the US dollar, the value of the stablecoin is linked to the value of the US dollar. Additionally, pegging is separate from the process of "backing." Pegging defines the value relationship of the coin. Backing, meanwhile, refers to the assets held in a secure vault by the issuer of the stablecoin; this is to ensure that there are enough funds to cover transactions and redemptions of the stablecoin.

Stablecoins came on the crypto scene in 2014 to reduce the volatility of cryptocurrencies and provide price stability. In 2018, the launch of USD Coin (USDC) increased regulatory interest in stablecoins. In 2021, there were several "failures" in the algorithm-based sector. The total losses were in the neighborhood of $40 billion. The failures pointed out the weak points in algorithmic-backed coins and began the process of targeted regulatory oversight and supervision of the space. The stablecoin realm has evolved and is now an important part of the crypto landscape.

TYPES OF STABLECOINS

There are four types of stablecoins:

- Fiat-backed stablecoins, which are backed by fiat currencies (such as the US dollar or euro).
- Commodity-backed stablecoins, which are backed by commodities (like gold and silver) held in the issuer's vault.
- Crypto-backed stablecoins, which are backed by other cryptocurrencies.
- Algorithm-backed stablecoins, which aim to maintain price stability via instructions on blockchain platforms that adjust the number of coins available in the system. Stablecoin prices that rise above the desired level instruct the algorithm to remove coins from the system. When the price falls below the desired level, the algorithm increases the number of coins in the system.

As you can see, all types are very different, and this book addresses all of them.

THE GENIUS ACT

The GENIUS Act (Guiding and Establishing National Innovation for US Stablecoins Act) is a US law passed in July 2025 to regulate stablecoins. Its goal is to protect consumers and increase transparency in the crypto market, and its central tenet requires stablecoins to be backed, one to one, by US dollars or other low-risk assets.

The passage of the GENIUS Act was followed by the passage of the Anti-Central Bank Digital Currency (CBDC) Surveillance State (H.R. 1919) Act, and the Digital Asset Market Clarity Act of 2025. The goal of the Anti-CBDC Surveillance State Act is to prevent the Federal Reserve from creating a central bank digital currency, while the Digital Asset Market Clarity Act divides supervision of digital assets between the Securities and Exchange Commission (SEC) and the Commodity Futures Trading Commission (CFTC).

Because of these three laws, the crypto space is likely to continue its evolution as both an asset class and a method of exchange. Over the next few years, crypto aficionados and the public at large can expect significant activity in the crypto universe.

That said, the crypto world has already worked toward creating a platform in which cryptocurrencies can evolve. The involvement of governments suggests that over the next few years, the lines will blur significantly between crypto and conventional currencies. Therefore, the following sections are a snapshot of where things stand in the present. Because the world of cryptocurrencies is inherently complex and rarely stands still, the future is almost certainly going to be a lot different than the present.

CONS OF DOLLAR- AND FIAT-BASED STABLECOINS

There's a major risk for the fiat dollar, and perhaps other major currencies. This is especially true of the US dollar, which is the world's reserve currency, but is also applicable to a lesser degree to the euro and the Japanese yen. That's because since they are widely accepted, reserve currencies act as a buffer for budget deficits. Thus, it's possible that stablecoins pegged to the major fiat currencies may distort the reserve currency effect (the tolerance that the world has for the fiscal policy of the reserve currency's country), and thus may affect the ability that the US, Europe, Japan, and others would not be able to run budget deficits to the same degree that they currently do. This is a bit of a difficult concept, but it's simplified by thinking of a reserve currency as a cushion (or a crutch) for governments to spend money because their currencies are reserve currencies. In other words, governments sometimes abuse their reserve currencies to spend more aggressively.

There are some other concerns worth noting. For example, there's the possibility of a financial crisis triggering a run on stablecoins, which could further increase the risks of a financial catastrophe extending to other markets (currencies, bonds, or stocks). There's also the risk that loopholes in legislation create a situation where the reserves are only present on paper and not in tangible terms (the reserves exist only as figures in a blockchain but aren't really there in the real world due to fraud or central bank error). Finally, there's further room for fraud or criminal use such as evading sanctions, fraudulent schemes, or money laundering. There's a lot that could go wrong, but all financial means have their upsides and downsides.

Worldwide Financial Crises

The risk of a major financial crisis is always present, in crypto or in the tangible world. All that's required are specific conditions lining up in a way that can trigger disorder. Consider the effect of the subprime mortgage crisis and the 2020 pandemic on the global financial system, where financial markets crashed and the money available in the system for transactions (also known as liquidity) dried up. Similar events could cripple the traditional financial system and spill into crypto as panic sets in and investors liquidate assets.

FIAT-COLLATERALIZED STABLECOINS: PART 1

Crypto Backed by Government-Issued Currency

Fiat-collateralized stablecoins are pegged to fiat currencies, such as the US dollar and the euro. Each is pegged on a 1:1 ratio to the underlying fiat. Thus, if a stablecoin (X) is pegged to the dollar, then 1X stablecoin = 1 US dollar. US dollar–pegged stablecoins make up over 99% of the stablecoin universe as of mid-2025.

Additionally, the legislative push in the US toward crypto and stablecoins becoming reserve tools for the US dollar aims to expand the role of the dollar as the world's reserve currency. So, the odds of stablecoins becoming mainstream financial assets are likely to increase steadily over time, barring extraordinary events.

There are five major dollar-backed stablecoins: Tether (USDT), USD Coin (USDC), USDS (previously known as DAI), Ethena USDe, and PayPal USD (PYUSD). This section (Part 1) covers Tether and the USD Coin.

TETHER (USDT)

Stablecoins are an attempt to dampen the price volatility inherent to the crypto asset class, and they're useful in conducting transactions due to their usually reliable price. Each stablecoin is pegged to an asset class, such as gold, the US dollar, commodities, and others. The most widely used stablecoin is Tether (USDT). The symbol USDT identifies Tether as the Tether stablecoin pegged to the US dollar. Its price fluctuates with the value of the dollar while simultaneously being backed by Tether's US dollar holdings.

Tether is owned by iFinex, a company housed in Hong Kong that owns the Bitfinex crypto exchange. Tether was launched in 2014, and its market cap in July 2025 was in the vicinity of $160 billion. Tether has expanded its stablecoin offerings with coins backed by the euro (EURT), the Mexican peso (MXNT), and the Chinese yuan (CNHT). In July 2025, Tether was trading at $1. You can buy Tether tokens on crypto exchanges such as Binance.

Unfortunately, iFinex has had multiple legal problems throughout the years. Tether faced regulatory scrutiny in 2021 for not consistently maintaining adequate reserves in its vault, and iFinex was also successfully hacked with $31 million worth of Tether being stolen. Since then, the company has resolved the issues and continued to grow.

Tether remains the most popular stablecoin. It's liquid, widely accepted, and considered the market standard. However, because iFinex is a Hong Kong–based Chinese company, there is always the chance that any economic or politically motivated policy changes in China, such as a trade war or military conflict with the US, may affect its operations.

Tether is supported by multiple blockchains including Tron, Ethereum, BNB Smart Chain, BitTorrent Chain, Avalanche, Fantom, Polygon, Arbitrum, Optimism, Aurora, and Aptos. Each deposit is verified by periodic audits, and despite having had some issues, iFinex is widely seen as adhering to US laws.

USD COIN

USD Coin (USDC) is the number two dollar-based coin. Housed in Boston, Massachusetts, it originated in 2013 when a consortium, including Wall Street giant Goldman Sachs, funded its beginnings through its management company Circle Internet Group. USD Coin is operated by both Circle and the Coinbase exchange. It is also liquid (an easy to transact asset) and has a solid reputation for strict adherence to US crypto and securities laws. It's supported by the Algorand, Arbitrum, Avalanche, Base, Celo, Ethereum, Hedera, NEAR, Noble, Optimism, Polkadot, Polygon, Solana, Stellar, Sui, and ZKsync blockchain platforms.

Unlike USDT, which is the native coin of the Tether platform, the USD Coin (USDC) is a separate entity, managed by a different company known as Circle. Both are stablecoins backed by and pegged to the US dollar. Each USD Coin is backed by an equal amount of dollars at regulated financial institutions while the reserve account is housed at the Bank of New York Mellon. And while their symbols (USDC and USDT) are similar, there are clear distinctions between these two stablecoins.

Here's how USD Coin works: When you buy 1 USDC, the money is deposited and stored by Circle and you own one coin equal to one US dollar. When you sell the coin, you get your dollar back, the coin is "burned," and your dollar is sent back to your bank account or your crypto wallet. USD Coin is compatible with Solana, Ethereum, and other platforms; it's also supported by both the Binance and Coinbase exchanges.

The major advantages of USD Coin are price stability and its backing by the US dollar. The major disadvantage is that there is no price appreciation (its value is always as close to $1 as possible), and because of its peg, it's vulnerable to the price changes of the US dollar, especially when the dollar falls in value, which can be an inflationary issue.

USD Coin offers a hedge against crypto's price volatility, especially during periods of market turmoil. During those periods, you may exchange your crypto holdings into USD Coin to avoid wide price fluctuations and preserve the value of your crypto portfolio. Foreign investors who want exposure to the US dollar can use the USD Coin without having to open traditional banking accounts.

To Convert or Not to Convert

USD Coin is a viable exchange mechanism for interacting in the crypto universe, but its lack of convertibility to bitcoin may be a bit cumbersome. That said, given its full convertibility to ether, you still have plenty of opportunities to use it as a method of payment as well as a storehouse of value for your crypto holdings.

FIAT-COLLATERALIZED STABLECOINS: PART 2

Other Important Alternatives

This section explores a subset of alternative stablecoins that offer their own advantages. Like Tether and the USD Coin, these coins are designed to offer a convenient method of value transfer while dampening the volatility inherent to traditional cryptocurrency prices.

USDS

USDS takes an interesting approach on the pegging theme: It offers a hybrid construct. It's predominantly traded on the Ethereum platform, which comes in handy if you're a fan of that platform. The coin was launched in 2024 by Sky, formerly known as MakerDAO, and is deployed via the Solana platform.

Its method of pegging its value to the dollar is different from other stablecoins, as it uses smart contracts, which adjust collateral levels automatically to maintain price stability. USDS is collateralized by other cryptocurrencies, not by dollars (thus the hybrid status; it's backed by crypto reserves, but pegged to the dollar). What this means is that this coin's value is 1:1 for every dollar, but the assets/reserves that back its liquidity are cryptocurrencies. USDS justifies its pegging and collateralizing method by noting that it allows the coin to operate independently of any single issuer, thus being more influenced by its community. In addition, its users can borrow, lend, and trade with USDS as the medium for these transactions outside of a centralized authority.

USDS collateral is held in banks, money market funds, and Bridge, a crypto services software company that specializes in crypto payment processing, which is owned by the online payment processing giant Stripe. Although USDS came into existence in November 2024, it has gained rapid acceptance and is considered the primary crypto-backed stablecoin—the third largest behind Tether and the USD Coin, with a market cap of nearly $9 billion in November 2025.

You can use USDS for lending and borrowing as well as a refuge from price volatility in coins in the Ethereum platform. The ability to exchange USDS for bitcoin varies per platform. If you're a bitcoin holder, it's a good idea to check which platforms allow this exchange before you open a wallet to convert your holdings to USDS.

USDE

USDe, also known as Ethena USDe is the stablecoin of the Ethena ecosystem. It's pegged to the US dollar 1:1, but its price stability is managed through a mechanism known as delta hedging, which involves options and derivative transactions based on cryptocurrency. Delta hedging is a two part strategy. First, each USDe coin is backed by crypto collateral. The second part of the strategy is that each coin is offset by a short position in derivatives (such as crypto futures). Combined, the two strategies aim to keep the price of USDe close to $1. Thus, there are no fiat, asset, or commodity reserves to back the peg or the price stability or value of the coin. USDe came onto the market in 2024. The market cap of USDe in August 2025 was in the vicinity of $12 billion, placing it in the top four stablecoins.

Here's how delta hedging works: Let's say you convert an ether coin to USDe. Your transaction triggers the exchange to sell derivatives, such as ETH futures contracts in an equal amount to cover the risk of loss and keep the price of USDe stable. The derivative sales (also known as short sales) produce income that is then accrued to your USDe tokens.

The strategy offers rewards to holders, in the form of interest-derived payments through the Ethereum-based Internet Bond Program, but it is dependent on the conditions of the derivative markets in which the hedging is done. Additionally, USDe holders can also receive rewards by staking (the practice of pledging tokens that won't be traded to maintain the stability of the blockchain). Staking of tokens often yields higher returns than treasury bonds from ETH-related collateral as well as other derivative-related sources. While this is a significant innovation, and the coin has gathered a faithful following, it's not without risk. If one or more of the counterparties involved in the derivative transactions becomes illiquid, the risk of loss will rise rapidly.

USDe is convertible to most other cryptocurrencies, although it's always good to get the full details with your exchange. So, if you're looking to earn high returns for holding a stablecoin, USDe fits the bill. It also offers a different level of risk than other stablecoins due to its reliance on the derivative (hedging by the short sale of crypto futures) market mechanism.

PAYPAL USD (PYUSD)

PayPal USD (PYUSD) is the first stablecoin launched by a US financial firm (PayPal) and is collateralized by US dollars, US treasuries, and dollar-based cash equivalents. It is pegged 1:1 to the US dollar. You can buy PayPal USD through the PayPal system.

What makes PayPal USD most attractive is that it can simplify crypto-based transactions made through the PayPal network. Don't view this as a guarantee of safety since the usual risks of crypto are applicable. However, given PayPal's ubiquitousness in the global financial system and the increased adoption of crypto as a storehouse of value and a method of financial transfers, PayPal USD is an interesting addition to the scene.

As a bonus, you can transfer PayPal USD to compatible crypto wallets in the PayPal system or externally. Originally, the coin's use was limited to the Ethereum and Solana platforms. Its deployment has expanded to multiple other platforms, including Ethereum's top Layer-2 blockchain Arbitrum, which is affiliated with the Robinhood trading app. You can buy products directly with PayPal USD, with the coin being automatically converted to fiat at the point of purchase. You can also trade PayPal USD for any PayPal-supported currency and earn rewards through its use.

Expect Growth in Collateralized Stablecoins

Collateralized stablecoins are likely to continue to multiply in number and in general scope. Over time, we will see further regulatory clarity and expanded acceptance into the mainstream financial system. Still, a major challenge facing this type of cryptocurrency is acceptance by the general public.

COMMODITY-BACKED STABLECOINS

Crypto Backed by Material Goods or Products

A commodity-backed stablecoin is pegged to the value of the underlying commodity, such as gold or silver. Commodity-backed currencies are redeemable in the underlying commodity and offer their users exposure to the underlying commodity via cryptocurrency. Commodity-backed stablecoins can be redeemed in the form of the underlying commodity.

Each token offers a 1:1 peg (claim) to a real commodity stored in an insured vault. The market value for commodity-backed stablecoins is significantly smaller than that for fiat-backed tokens (less than 1% of all stablecoins), but the value of the sector has risen and is likely to rise further while commodity prices rise.

The advantage of commodity-backed stablecoins is that they are pegged to something tangible; they offer potential physical access to precious metals without necessarily holding them physically. This is a direct contrast to other methods of exposure to metals, such as exchange-traded funds (ETFs) or mutual funds. However, there are downsides like storage costs and custodial/processing fees, which are assessed upon redemption. There's also lower liquidity compared to fiat-backed stablecoins.

PAX GOLD (PAXG)

The leading commodity-backed stablecoin is Pax Gold (PAXG), through which token holders gain access to one troy ounce (31.1

grams) of gold per coin. The gold that backs the coin is a London Bullion Market Association (LBMA)–accredited vault in London. Pax Gold was launched by Paxos, a New York–based crypto brokerage and financial services that manages the custody of the gold. It is regulated by the New York State Department of Financial Services and produces a monthly audit by accounting firm KPMG.

You can own portions of a coin (0.01 ounces for approximately $20) on Ethereum. You can also redeem your Pax Gold for real gold bullion in several forms. Pax Gold is supported on Ethereum, the Binance Smart Chain (BSC), Solana, and Arbitrum. You'll be charged a fee for redeeming the gold.

TETHER GOLD (XAUT)

Tether Gold tokens offer ownership of physical gold stored in Swiss vaults. As with Pax Gold, each Tether Gold token spots the ownership of one LBMA-accredited troy ounce of gold. Tether Gold is a slightly smaller portion of the gold-backed coins than Pax Gold based on market capitalization, though both are in the $1 billion range.

The pros and cons of Tether Gold are similar to those of Pax Gold. As with Pax Gold, Tether Gold is highly accessible to retail and individual investors as its tradeable on the Ethereum, Tron, and TON platforms. However, redemption for gold bars is limited to Switzerland, and associated fees apply. Additionally, the audits for Tether Gold are less frequent than those for Pax Gold, which leaves a lot of goodwill on the part of investors to trust the Tether platform.

KINESIS (KAU)

Kinesis is a much smaller coin by market cap, somewhere near one-tenth of the value of Tether Gold and Pax Gold. Whereas the other two have finite storage places for the backing gold (London for Pax Gold and Switzerland for Tether Gold), Kinesis allows its gold to be stored in audited, accredited vaults around the world.

Each Kinesis represents one gram of "fine" gold (0.995, or 99.5% purity) and is redeemable for no less than a 100-gram, LBMA-approved gold bar. You can trade and transact using Kinesis via the Kinesis Virtual Card, which is accepted where Mastercard is accepted. When you use your Kinesis Virtual Card, you earn rewards. It self-conducts biannual audits, and its use is limited to the Kinesis platform.

KINESIS SILVER (KAG)

Kinesis Silver tokens are backed by one troy ounce of "fine" silver (silver that is 99.9% pure) that is stored and insured in independently audited vaults around the world. The tokens are issued by Kinesis Money and are managed through the Allocated Bullion Exchange (ABX).

You can redeem Kinesis Silver for as little as 200 ounces housed throughout the world. Kinesis Silver pays holders' dividends accrued through a fee sharing arrangement in the community. Beginners should be aware that the price of silver can be more volatile than the price of gold, and that a bull market in gold isn't always correspondent to a bull market in silver. Kinesis Silver is also less liquid than gold-backed stablecoins.

MATRIXDOCK GOLD (XAUM)

Matrixdock Gold is a regional gold-backed stablecoin mostly appealing to Asian marketplaces, as the backing gold is stored mainly in Singapore and Hong Kong. It offers ownership of LBMA-backed gold similar to Pax Gold and Tether Gold. Plus, with this platform, you can group multiple Matrixdock Gold tokens into NFTs representing specific gold bars. You can receive physical delivery of gold held via Matrixdock Gold, but this is a small operation by comparison to the larger players, and thus has smaller liquidity.

VENEZUELA'S PETRO

There is one crude oil–backed stablecoin known as the Petro. It is issued by oil-rich Venezuela and is "backed" by the country's oil reserves. Unfortunately, due to the volatile political and economic situation in the country, combined with the uncertain aspects of the actual access to the oil reserves, the Petro has failed to gain traction. It is not listed on any major exchange. There have been other attempts to create crude oil–backed stablecoins, but none have gone very far.

Importance of Collateral

When it comes to stablecoins, it's important to note that a significant portion of a coin owner's trust is based on the audits that verify the existence and accuracy of the collateral that back the stability of the underlying coin. While auditors are mostly honest in their work, they can certainly be duped. Therefore, if a stablecoin is not audited by a "credible" auditor, it's best to avoid it.

CRYPTO-BACKED STABLECOINS

Increased Complexity with a Built-In Safety Net

One factor that sets crypto apart from other financial sectors is its relative "newness" in the system and the fact that it's still evolving. Now enter crypto-backed stablecoins. The next step in the evolution of stablecoins is the validation of crypto itself via its use as a backing mechanism for stablecoins. This type of stablecoin actually collateralizes one form of crypto with another. And although that sounds flimsy at first, fiat currencies are backed by the "legal tender" promise of a government that they're "good for it." So, what makes this any different?

Yes, the dollar is the world's reserve currency because the US government "backs" it with its word. You can say the same about the euro, the yen, the yuan, and the Swiss franc, among others. Certainly, in a more abstract sense, the US economy is the de facto "backer" of the US dollar. But a fiat currency is one that can (and often is) be printed out of thin air by central banks when conditions call for it, such as during the pandemic when the Federal Reserve printed trillions of dollars via its Quantitative Easing (QE) Program. This makes crypto backing other crypto coins look more legitimate.

That said, crypto-backed stablecoins maintain their value by being collateralized by other crypto coins. So, the potential for volatility increases with this type of stablecoin. The backing cryptocurrency is known as the reserve cryptocurrency (the "we're good for it" coin), which may be a very volatile coin such as bitcoin (BTC).

PROS AND CONS OF CRYPTO-BACKED STABLECOINS

The allure of crypto-backed stablecoins is the decentralization of your money—the ability to make transactions without a third party (such as a government or private banking institution). Transactions are deemed easier to execute since the entire process is blockchain based. Moreover, there is often more liquidity in the crypto-based stablecoins than in fiat or commodity-based coins.

The downside is that the system is more complex, and that the number of coins in circulation may be more volatile than other stablecoin realms. Finally, the stability of the system is dependent on the collateralization of the stablecoin, as described in this entry.

THE PROOF OF RESERVES AUDIT

Because of the inherent risk of backing one form of crypto with another, there are safeguards in place to maintain an orderly flow in the trading and transaction activities of crypto-backed stablecoins. The first is the Proof of Reserves report, whose function is to prove that a cryptocurrency exchange has enough assets to cover all of its customers' deposits. This assures transparency and inspires confidence in users of the exchange. It is backed by the Proof of Reserves audit, an audit that verifies that a cryptocurrency exchange does in fact have enough assets to cover customer deposits.

The Proof of Reserves audit is accomplished via a data analytics structure known as a Merkle Tree, which is available through a mechanism known as the Merkle Root. The Merkle Root is a tamper-proof crypto fingerprint of reserves that auditors can access to verify their results. This data is secure and difficult—though not completely impossible—to falsify.

By the same token, the Proof of Reserves audit is a snapshot, not an ongoing dynamic verification process. Thus, a good audit for the present does not guarantee a good audit for the future. In other words, if a crypto company wants to hide something, it can do so via "off the books" assets or even bribing the auditing team.

A Stablecoin's Balance Sheet

Think of the Proof of Reserves data as a glimpse into the balance sheet of the crypto entity's ability to back the stablecoin. It has some limitations, but it's much better than nothing. This system is also likely to evolve over time as new regulations are applied.

THE OVER-COLLATERALIZATION PARADIGM

The second safety net in the crypto-backed stablecoin realm is the practice of over-collateralization. That's the process by which there are more reserves available to back the stablecoin than the value of all the stablecoins in the system. The ratio varies, and the form of reserves may include more than one backup crypto. For example, MakerDao's DAI dollar-pegged stablecoin is backed by Ethereum and other cryptocurrencies with a value of 155% of the DAI coins in circulation.

SKY'S USDS AND SKY GOVERNANCE TOKEN (SKY)

The Benchmark of Crypto-Backed Coins

The USDS stablecoin and the Sky Governance Token (formerly Maker token) are the most liquid and are considered the prototype for the crypto-backed stablecoin realm. The Sky platform's primary function is to provide a lending mechanism to its users. Lenders receive interest, and borrowers receive funds that can be used for trading or other transactions, such as business expansions and debt servicing.

USDS is the native coin of the Sky ecosystem, whereas the Sky token is the governing token through which the platform ensures that DAI maintains a value close to $1, and a voting mechanism through which the platform's direction is controlled by its users.

ABOUT SKY AND USDS

In September 2024, MakerDAO changed its name to Sky in order to rebrand and upgrade its operations. The USDS stablecoin was introduced by Sky after its rebranding. Thus, the DAI stablecoin was renamed (rebranded) and evolved into the USDS stablecoin in the new Sky platform. The Maker token was renamed the Sky Governance Token (SKY). Governance tokens are cryptocurrencies that allow users of a platform to vote on how the platform is run. DAI is no longer minted, and holders who wish to hold on to the legacy coins can do so, or they can exchange it for USDS on a 1:1 basis. The conversion rate for Maker to Sky is 1 MKR = 24,000 SKY.

The Sky platform is a decentralized finance (DeFi) blockchain protocol that operates inside the Ethereum platform, but it may expand to other blockchains in the future. This platform allows users to lend and borrow cryptocurrencies. (Remember: DeFi is a system that allows financial transactions via the execution of smart contracts without third parties being involved.) USDS is pegged to the dollar on a 1:1 basis, and it's backed by cryptocurrency deposits that are secured by the practice of over-collateralization and several other mechanisms described in detail in this entry.

USING THE PLATFORMS

MakerDAO started by allowing users to deposit ether to generate the DAI stablecoin; Sky has since expanded its operation to include other Ethereum-based tokens. To obtain crypto-backed loans on this platform, you buy other cryptos for collateral and pay them back in USDS through a mechanism (smart contract) known as the collateralized debt position (CDP). This is an arrangement between you and the decentralized application (dApp), a software application that resides in the protocol and executes smart contracts.

After the system verifies that you have enough collateral deposited, it prints the number of tokens required for completing the transaction. The CDP is then locked in Sky's vaults until the debt is repaid. You can use the borrowed tokens to trade, hedge, to buy other cryptocurrencies, or to earn interest on other protocols.

Because of the over-collateralization in the system, if a user wanted to buy $100,000 of USDS or SKY tokens, they would have to provide collateral in the amount of whatever the operating requirement is at the time. For example, if the requirement is 150%, you'd have to put up $150,000 of crypto, such as ether, to complete the transaction. If you can't pay the loan on time, like when your collateral drops below the value of your investment, you will face automatic liquidation of your holdings.

Over-Collateralization

Over-collateralization is a built-in safety net for cryptocurrencies, reducing the risk of cryptocurrency's price volatility to lending mechanisms used by platforms. By requiring an amount of collateral that exceeds the loan's value, over-collateralization reduces the chances of losses to lenders. An equally important aspect of the practice is that it maintains the stability of the platform via its risk reduction.

USDS'S STABILITY CLAIM AND DOWNSIDE

USDS is deemed as a reliable stablecoin due to its relative longevity (it was created in 2014). In addition to its over-collateralization, it's considered a reliable method of value retention due to:

- Its ability to survive several periods of instability in the crypto universe.
- Its levying of stability fees, which it garners when new USDS tokens are created. The fees are paid via SKY tokens and are

variable depending on whether the value of USDS rises or falls below $1.

- The process of SKY dilution through which Sky mints new tokens to increase the number of tokens available for purchasing when token liquidations exceed levels that affect the value of USDS.

Finally, you should know that the transaction time may be slow. Liquidity may also be strained during periods of severe market volatility, such as what users experienced during the pandemic in 2020.

Governance Tokens Offer Users a Voice in How Platforms Are Run

Governance tokens are integral parts of cryptocurrency platforms, as they allow the users to provide their input into how the platform operates via a transparent mechanism. Their use ranges in decisions that can include important events, from proposed software updates to the platform to protocol changes. Votes are influenced by the number of tokens held by each individual on the platform. The flip side is that the tokens are widely distributed.

WRAPPED BITCOIN (WBTC)

The Bridge Between Bitcoin and Ethereum

Wrapped bitcoin (WBTC) is an important crypto-backed stablecoin. It was launched in 2019 by a collaboration between several large players in crypto, including custodian BitGo and DeFi protocol network Kyber Network. It was developed as a way to expand the potential for the use of bitcoin outside of the Bitcoin blockchain without compromising the built-in uniqueness and security of the blockchain.

ABOUT WRAPPED BITCOIN

Wrapped bitcoin is a tokenized version of bitcoin (BTC); it is pegged 1:1 to the value of bitcoin, and it trades on the Ethereum platform, but it can also be used on multiple platforms for lending, borrowing, and trading of other cryptocurrencies. It's widely used and sometimes referred to as "digital gold" because it offers bitcoin holders access to the DeFi benefits of the Ethereum system, such as apps and lending. These features are not available on the Bitcoin system while accessing the size, reach, and liquidity of bitcoin.

RENBTC AND STACKS BTC

There are two similar Ethereum-blockchain, bitcoin-based tokens, which should be mentioned to avoid confusion and clarify significant differences between them and wrapped bitcoin. renBTC is issued by the Ren protocol and is also a 1:1 equivalent of bitcoin, allowing bitcoin users to transact on the Ethereum blockchain. There are some differences in converting bitcoin to renBTC when compared to the ease of transferring value to wrapped bitcoin. Moreover, there are some smart contract vulnerabilities related to renBTC that can potentially increase the security risk.

Another offshoot is Stacks bitcoin (sBTC), established in late 2024, which is issued and managed by the Stacks protocol. Rather than using a custodian-based system, Stacks bitcoin moves freely between the Stacks and Bitcoin blockchains. The value of Stacks bitcoin is essentially the same as that of bitcoin because its peg is 1:1 to bitcoin. However, its advantage is that Stacks bitcoin transactions are conducted in the Bitcoin blockchain, which offers the liquidity and security of bitcoin to the Stacks bitcoin assets.

MINTING WRAPPED BITCOIN

Minting is the process of creating new coins by authenticating data, the creation of new blocks, and the subsequent recording of the information on the blockchain. Minting uses the proof of stake (PoS) protocol. To mint wrapped bitcoins, you send bitcoins to a custodian (merchant) such as BitGo. This merchant mints wrapped bitcoins, which correspond to your transfer on a 1:1 basis through a smart contract; this contract preserves the value of the original coins and transfers to the wrapped tokens. The bitcoins deposited are then "custodied" by the merchant, where there is transparency and accountability. The newly minted tokens are then attributed to the owner. Once the process is completed, you can then use your newly minted wrapped bitcoins. To redeem, you contact the custodian and burn (removing crypto tokens from circulation in order to increase the value of the tokens that remain in circulation) the tokens, which converts them to bitcoins.

Wrapped bitcoin is highly liquid, ultimately expanding the liquidity of the DeFi space. As a result, the process leads to faster transactions than what you see in the traditional Bitcoin space. This stablecoin also expands the use of bitcoin by allowing other activities to happen, such as yield farming.

Important Differences Between Bitcoin and Wrapped Bitcoin

As with many issues in cryptocurrency, terminology and design can lead to confusion. So, while bitcoin is the prototype cryptocurrency, wrapped bitcoin is a tokenized version of bitcoin. Its primary use is to bring the liquidity of bitcoin to the Ethereum and related DeFi platforms. In other words, it forms a bridge that allows users to transact on Ethereum based on the value of their bitcoins.

Here are the important differences between bitcoin and wrapped bitcoin:

- Bitcoin was created in 2009. Wrapped bitcoin was created in 2019.
- Wrapped bitcoin was designed to expand the use of bitcoin to other platforms such as Ethereum and Ethereum-based DeFi platforms, including the use of linked apps and smart contracts.
- Wrapped bitcoin transactions tend to be faster based on the operation of the Ethereum platform.
- Wrapped bitcoin transactions are likely to have lower costs than traditional bitcoin transactions.

- Bitcoin is self-custodied by individuals in their private wallets where they hold the keys. Wrapped bitcoins are centrally custodied by members of the wrapped token decentralized autonomous organization (DAO)—most commonly BitGo. Thus, when users mint wrapped bitcoins, they must deposit the corresponding number of bitcoins with the custodian.
- The supply of bitcoin is limited to 21 million coins by design. In contrast, wrapped bitcoins are minted only when users deposit bitcoins with a merchant, who then initiates the custodian process via BitGo.
- While bitcoin is used primarily as a storehouse of value and an investment, wrapped bitcoin's frequent uses include lending and borrowing, derivatives trading (futures and options), and bitcoin-related staking mechanisms.
- Wrapped bitcoin's liquidity is limited to DeFi platforms, while bitcoin is more widely accepted.

These differences help with giving bitcoin and wrapped bitcoin their own advantages and disadvantages. Both are good coins; which one is better for you to acquire depends on your portfolio.

THE ELECTRONIC US DOLLAR (EUSD)

The First Data-Processing Cryptocurrency

The Electronic US Dollar (eUSD) stablecoin is a niche, but steadily growing, stablecoin that operates on the Reserve Protocol ecosystem, a platform designed for "stability and decentralization" of money backed by Silicon Valley heavyweights, including Peter Thiel and Sam Altman. The platform's goal is to create a fully decentralized banking system. The Reserve Protocol allows anyone to create or modify a fully asset-backed stablecoin. eUSD is the "official" token of the Reserve Protocol.

Electronic USD (eUSD) is officially described as a data-processing stablecoin; it functions on an end-to-end zero-knowledge encryption system where only the two ends of the transaction, the sender and receiver, can see the transaction details, thus ensuring privacy. Moreover, Electronic USD does not store any transactional data, again ensuring that only the users involved have access to the data. At the same time, Electronic USD complies with all pertinent regulations, including the Know Your Customer (KYC) and anti-money laundering (AML) rules.

Electronic USD is a unique stablecoin, pegged 1:1 to the US dollar and functions on the Reserve and MobileCoin platforms. It's backed by a basket of stablecoins, including USD Coin and Tether. Moreover, it's over-collateralized by staked (locked and validated) Reserve Rights (RSR) tokens—the governance token of the Reserve Protocol—that allows holders to vote on protocol changes on the platform. To add another layer of safety, Reserve offers 24/7 continuous on-chain proof of reserves access. This allows users to monitor the status of reserves on the blockchain and reduces the potential distortions and censorship that can be present when one or more users hold a large majority of tokens. Staked RSR tokens also allow holders to earn a share of the revenue generated by the tokens while acting as a backstop in case of token defaults. Plus, on Ethereum, Electronic USD is linked to Reserve's liquidity pools to offer access to yield-generating opportunities to Electronic USD holders. On MobileCoin, transactions are completed rapidly with low, uniform fees regardless of the size of the transactions and a high level of privacy.

A staked RSR token is deposited into a staking contract built around a decentralized token folio (DTF) on individual platforms (a DTF is a crypto version of an exchange-traded fund [ETF]). The holder then receives payment tokens housed in the DTF. DTFs will index multiple crypto assets into a single portfolio.

Electronic USD is pegged 1:1 to the US dollar via an over-collateralized basket of yield-bearing stablecoins, including USD Coin and Tether. On Ethereum, the proof of reserves is available 24/7, allowing auditing and transparency. Electronic USD is usable on the MobileCoin ecosystem with rapid transaction times (5 seconds) and low transaction fees ($0.0025 eUSD).

BUILT-IN SAFETY AND USEFULNESS

Because the Reserve Protocol is decentralized, it's less liable to be hacked or internally corrupted, thus lessening the chances of fraud and censorship. This is accomplished by the verification of each transaction by multiple nodes (computers operating within the system) before finalization.

The peg to the US dollar makes Electronic USD convenient for retail transactions or as a saving mechanism. It offers low-fee international transfers ($0.00256 eUSD/payment) and offers access through specialized apps such as Sentz. Finally, with Electronic USD, you have instant access to your funds, although the mechanism varies by country.

You can use Electronic USD for many transactions, including global payments, e-commerce, and remittances. You can also stake or pool Electronic USD to generate income, often at a higher interest rate than you may receive in the conventional banking system.

Staking Electronic USD

When you stake your Electronic USD, you're locking it up in a wallet where it's used by the platform as part of the security of the platform. The platform pays you for your assistance via tokens, which over time add up and increase your crypto holdings with less risk than you would incur by trading. Moreover, if applicable, your staked tokens allow you to participate in the governance of the platform through applicable operation-related votes that may come up.

To proceed with staking, you need to create an account at a chosen platform that supports Electronic USD. Then, you need to set up your wallet (either by creating a new wallet or connecting to an existing wallet). Finally, you must provide enough funds, in accordance with the platform's requirements, to begin staking.

Once you've set up your account and funded your wallet, review the available options for staking Electronic USD. You can choose a staking pool, and you should check out its performance. Choose the pool that balances consistent results with higher reward levels. Always review the fees involved, and don't forget to check out the pool's reputation in community posts. The final step is to enter the amount you're staking and hit the "Delegate" button, which locks up your Electronic USD for staking. After you confirm the transaction, make sure you track your rewards and see if they meet your expectations. If you're not satisfied, you can move your Electronic USD to another pool that offers better results.

So Many Crypto-Backed Stablecoins

The crypto-backed stablecoin universe is rapidly growing. Each platform often has its own version of the same coin. It's always important to do further research in order to fully understand the ins and outs of how each coin, and the platform-specific version of each coin, functions.

SEIGNIORAGE (ALGORITHMIC)-BACKED STABLECOINS

Cryptocurrency Stabilized by Algorithms

The last category of stablecoins is that of seigniorage (algorithmic)-backed stablecoins, which are backed by algorithms instead of US dollars, gold, silver, or other cryptocurrencies. These are sometimes called algo-backed coins. They are backed by smart contracts designed to reduce price volatility by adjusting the supply of the token to bring the price back to the 1:1 peg, usually to the US dollar. As a potential user, you must be able to balance the positives of this type of coin, which include their transparency based on their auditable code, and their major downside: They are often under-collateralized and thus risky, even by crypto standards.

Algo-backed coins are the most controversial subsector of the stablecoin realm and are not meant for beginners. Of course, the allure of anonymity while making transactions and the potential elation of avoiding third-party fees is certainly on their side. However, because of collateralization, you should avoid this sector until you're more experienced.

HOW ALGO-BACKED STABLECOINS WORK

The backing algorithm actively manages supply and demand for the coin via smart contracts, which keeps the price stable—usually at $1.

So, if the price falls below $1, the algorithm reduces the number of tokens in the system to bring the price back up. If the price rises above $1, the algorithm mints tokens or offers incentives to the system to increase the number of tokens and thus bring the price back to $1.

Algo-backed systems often use two separate tokens to achieve price stability. One token is deemed to be stable, while the second is volatile and is used to "absorb" market risk and restore stability. Again, there's no tangible backing asset. Indeed, the most famous algo-backed coin failure, TerraUSD (UST), is known for its 2022 collapse as the combination of fraudulent activity by the creators and the lack of tangible asset backup led to the downfall of its ecosystem, resulting in a $60 billion loss.

AMPLEFORTH (AMPL)

Because crypto has nine lives, even after the TerraUSD debacle, there are still algo-backed stablecoins available, at least as of this writing. One of them is Ampleforth (AMPL), that has a market cap of less than $35 million and a volatile price which, as of this writing, is above $1. That said, Ampleforth is designed to be resistant to supply inflation and is decoupled from the price of other cryptocurrencies, especially Bitcoin. Instead of holding individual coins, ownership of Ampleforth is deployed via a percentage of the supply of tokens available.

When the algorithm detects the supply is too high, it decreases the supply of tokens (a process known as "contracting supply") and this change in supply is propagated throughout the wallets of all holders by an adjustment of the price, not by tampering with the number of tokens owned by users. To keep the price at $1, Ampleforth deploys a process called a "rebase." It happens once per day with the baseline adjustments occurring when prices rise above $1.06 or fall below $0.96. But don't worry, you still hold the same portion of the supply that you had before the adjustment. For illustrative purposes, as of this writing, the twenty-four-hour high price was $1.40. After the "debase," it fell to $1.21, meaning another debase is likely.

Other interesting Ampleforth facts to consider include:

- The supply of tokens is unlimited based on the price of the coin. Prices above $1 increase circulation, while prices under $1 decrease it.
- Ampleforth is "secured" via its association to the Ethereum blockchain and by the presence of "oracles," or data feeds from third parties, such as major crypto exchanges, which provide "off-chain" (data and information that occur outside of the blockchain, such as weather, sports, or specific transactions that may be pertinent to the blockchain) information to the blockchain. The blockchain then incorporates the information into its smart contracts.
- Ampleforth tends to be volatile, which is contrary to the "stable" expectations of the stablecoin realm.

Algo-backed stablecoins could gain wide acceptance. However, they do face a bit of an uphill climb given the public's familiarity with the US dollar and gold as traditional backing assets for currencies.

HYBRID ALGO-BACKED COINS

The Frax USD (frxUSD) is a fiat-redeemable and fully collateralized stablecoin issued by the Frax Finance Protocol. Frax USD was formerly known as Frax. This coin is a hybrid because its custodian mints or redeems the tokens based on collateral (cash and cash equivalent) reserves in its vaults while also adjusting the token supply via its underlying algorithm. Frax USD uses enshrined custodians (custodians approved by the platform). These are reliable entities whose function is to safeguard your crypto holdings by safeguarding your crypto wallet.

The enshrined custodian of your Frax USD holdings performs several functions, such as depositing your purchase in your wallet or burning legacy coins and depositing the proceeds of the burning in your wallet. The exchange is based on the price of $1 per coin and is transferred on a 1:1 basis. All transactions are based on the collateral in reserves in the custodian's vault.

New custodians can be added depending on Frax USD governance directives, and each custodian is assigned a cap on the number of reserves it's allowed to mint. This is accomplished via a Frax USD custodian contract. There are some interesting loopholes as well, known as whitelists—lists of "preferred wallets" that are allowed to participate in special events such as new token offerings. There are rules to govern who is allowed to be included in a whitelist. The take home message, however, is that members of whitelists receive special treatment such as access to ICOs and other perks. This process is a potential distortion mechanism in the supply and demand of cryptocurrencies but is unfortunately part of the landscape.

It's also important to note that if for whatever reason, a particular custodian is unable to redeem your token, another custodian entity with the available funds will redeem your token.

Future of Stablecoins

Stablecoins are still in their early evolutionary phase. Yet, because they bring price stability and increase the ease of making transactions to the world of cryptocurrencies, they are likely to become an integral part of the landscape over time.

Chapter 4

Using Cryptocurrency

Though there are many skeptics regarding the crypto world's long-term viability, there's no denying its presence in the economic market. The total value of the cryptocurrency market in November 2025 was over $3.5 trillion. That's roughly one and one-half the number of US dollars in circulation—$2.4 trillion. Indeed, cryptocurrencies are likely a permanent part of the financial world, and over time, they will become equally influential in the real world.

The wide acceptance of the asset class by large corporations and a growing presence in the financial markets have brought governments into the mix, which signals that an important milestone has been reached. The next logical step is the incorporation of cryptocurrency into the mainstream economy as a routine method of paying for daily necessities. This chapter explores the complexities of using cryptocurrencies as vehicles of transferring value. You'll start with the basics of where and how to set up accounts and finish with the particulars of how to use crypto for payment and gaining rewards through staking.

CRYPTO EXCHANGES

Where the Action Takes Place

Crypto exchanges are digital platforms that allow their users to buy, sell, trade, and conduct transactions with cryptocurrency as the value transferring method. They perform similar functions to a stock exchange. There are two types: centralized and decentralized exchanges. This entry focuses on three reliable exchanges that you can use as a starting point for choosing an exchange.

CENTRALIZED AND DECENTRALIZED EXCHANGES

Centralized exchanges, are centrally run with rules that govern transactions. Users are required to set up accounts, and the exchange provides customer support and trading options. The three largest centralized exchanges are Coinbase, Gemini, and Binance.

Decentralized exchanges allow users to trade directly. No central authority is involved. Users attracted to anonymity and control of their own funds often choose these. Popular decentralized exchanges include Uniswap and PancakeSwap.

In summary, centralized exchanges are intermediaries between buyers and sellers, are more user-friendly and resemble traditional discount brokers. Decentralized exchanges are more difficult to navigate but offer more anonymity via peer-to-peer trading.

When evaluating the exchange types, it's important to keep these key points in mind:

- Decentralized exchanges can be challenging for beginners because sometimes their trading dashboards can be difficult to manage as well as the existing potential for low liquidity during volatile trading periods.
- Centralized exchanges may have stronger security and may be insured.
- Decentralized exchanges may have lower fees, while centralized exchanges support a larger variety of tokens.

The rest of this entry focuses on prominent crypto exchanges business: Binance, Coinbase, and Kraken, as they are best suited (user-friendly) for beginners.

BINANCE

Binance is a centralized exchange. Established in 2017, it originated in China, migrated to Japan, and then to Malta to avoid government interference with its operations. By 2018, Binance was the largest crypto exchange based on trading volume; in 2019, it launched trading platforms for the euro and British pound (Binance Jersey). It has over 270 million users in over 180 countries.

In 2021, Binance was investigated by the US Department of Justice and the IRS for alleged connections to money laundering. In 2022, reports surfaced supporting criminal activity. The fraud stemmed from a criminal scheme started in 2019 and 2020 by a North Korean hacker group that used the exchange to sell drugs and launder money via making trades on the exchange. In 2023, Binance pled guilty in federal court to money laundering and unlicensed money transmitting. Its founder Changpeng Zhao was also convicted, paid a fine, and served a short prison term. Binance operates through multiple global offices and has had no further legal problems since 2023.

Binance Services
Binance offers a wide variety of services to users:

- Buying and selling cryptocurrencies including through credit, debit cards, bank transfers, or peer-to-peer (P2P) trading.
- Earning interest on your crypto holdings via staking and savings accounts.
- Lower fees compared to other exchanges.
- Spot trading of over 500 cryptocurrencies, including Bitcoin, Ethereum, and others.
- Margin trading of cryptocurrencies.
- Cryptocurrency futures and options trading.
- Participation in new token offerings to earn rewards (Launchpool).

Through Binance, you can set up your crypto wallet and you can add your own trading programs into their apps. Binance also offers educational materials on cryptocurrency and blockchain technology through Binance Academy. Binance also offers users access price charts and technical indicators. Price charts help users analyze price trends and to pinpoint entry and exit points when trading crypto.

Binance leverages its size and its market presence to provide lower fees and extensive services to its clients. Its security is seen as more advanced than other exchanges, as it offers two-factor authentication and cold storage, an advanced method of protecting users' private keys offline to prevent hacking. Binance also provides FDIC insurance for US dollars. The insurance only covers US dollars not invested in crypto.

COINBASE

Coinbase is the largest US-based crypto exchange. It's primarily a centralized exchange, while offering decentralized exchange transactions through its app. Its origin dates back to 2012 when it was founded by Brian Armstrong, the current CEO, and Fred Ehrsam. Armstrong's background is in economics and computer programming. Ehrsam is a former Goldman Sachs trader and founder of the Paradigm investment firm.

Coinbase serves some 110 million users, with 8 million users doing transactions on the platform per month. In its May 1, 2025, quarterly report, Coinbase held $328 billion total cryptocurrency assets under custody. In 2020, the figure was $90 billion. The average trading volume on Coinbase is approximately $3.5 billion as of August 2025.

Coinbase Global, Inc. is a publicly traded company, under the Nasdaq symbol COIN. The initial public offering (IPO), where the private company sold stock to the public, occurred in 2021. As of August 2025, its market cap was nearly $80 billion; for the 2025 fiscal year, it reported a yearly revenue of $7–$9 billion. Because it's a publicly traded company based in the US, it's highly regulated. This is a positive thing, as its financial status is highly believable due to the SEC oversight of publicly traded companies. For its

September 30, 2025, quarter, the company reported $433 million in net income.

Coinbase services both retail and institutional investors, offering services ranging from buying and selling over 200 cryptocurrencies (as of August 2025), an advanced trading platform, and access to NFTs, self-custody wallets, e-commerce business payments, and prepaid cards.

Its US-based regulatory structure offers its clients an institutional safety net. Its financial growth and expanding user base, and its wide array of services, certainly make it worth considering.

KRAKEN

Kraken is a lesser known but rapidly growing centralized exchange. Kraken was founded in 2011 by Jesse Powell, who got his start in the video game industry. Kraken is recognized for its safety features, its easy-to-use trading platform, and its broad access to over 400 cryptocurrencies.

Kraken was among the first crypto exchanges listed on the famed Bloomberg Terminal trading system, widely used by pros. Like Binance, it's had its share of regulatory issues; in 2023, the SEC sued the company for operating as an unlicensed exchange. To be fair, this is not an uncommon issue in crypto as the regulatory environment continues to evolve. The SEC dropped the lawsuit in 2025. Otherwise, Kraken has kept out of other major "issues" regarding potential criminal behavior.

Kraken offers two-factor authentication and uses cold wallets (offline wallets) to protect against hacks. Kraken offers users access to over 200 cryptocurrencies via spot trading (based solely on the current money in the account), margin trading (trading with borrowed money from the exchange), options and futures trading (derivative trades, more suitable for experienced traders; you can find more information on this in Chapter 6) through both its online platform and trading app for iPhones and Android phones. Its user interface is simple to operate for both beginners and experienced traders. Kraken offers lower fees for active traders and free trading plans for those who subscribe ($4.99 per month or $49.99 per year). You can trade on Kraken through money housed in your wallet or via prepayment cards.

Centralized Exchanges Are Beginner-Friendly

When starting out, consider a centralized exchange, which offers more support. Once you've gained some experience, consider decentralized exchanges, such as Uniswap, PancakeSwap, and SushiSwap, which allow peer-to-peer trading directly from your wallet.

HOT WALLETS

Your Online Crypto Bank Accounts

A crypto wallet is a holding place for your private crypto keys, the blockchain "passwords" that let you access your crypto assets and make crypto-mediated transactions. They can be housed online (hot wallets) or on external devices known as hardware wallets, similar in concept to USB or thumb drives. Other wallet types like cold wallets, mobile wallets, and custodial wallets are explained later in this chapter. Ultimately, hot wallets, which are independent of exchanges, have higher risk profiles because they are online. The other wallets all have their own benefits as well.

Before transacting in cryptocurrencies, you must set up a wallet in order to have a place to launch your crypto transactions. When you make a transaction, the private key is stored in your wallet. A private key is an access code that gives you access to your crypto assets; it is an encrypted alphanumeric number that is generated by the wallet, which confirms your ownership of the cryptocurrency and authorizes transactions. If someone steals your private key, the crypto associated with it is gone. If you lose your private key, you don't have access to your assets. That means that choosing the right type of wallet, based on your crypto goals and your risk tolerance, is extremely important.

ABOUT HOT WALLETS

A hot wallet is always connected to the Internet. They're basically crypto bank accounts—their function is to store, send, and receive tokens. They are convenient, as they're designed to allow personal access to your keys with fewer steps, but they're more vulnerable to hacks than offline wallets. They also require regular updates and maintenance for security. Some offer the ability to interact with cold wallets, thus offering a bit more security.

So, if you're an active crypto trader, or frequently interact with dApps, the hot wallet makes sense for you. However, because each wallet is different, it's important to research each one and to consider the possibility that you may need a different wallet for each type of cryptocurrency, or each specific group of cryptocurrencies you may wish to transact in.

There are many hot wallets available for use. This section focuses on two that are representative of what's available and provides the pros and cons of the entire group.

COINBASE WALLET

The Coinbase Wallet is a self-custody crypto wallet from Coinbase, where users have complete control of their private keys. In these wallets, the user is solely responsible for the management and security of their digital assets. The Coinbase Wallet is a separate entity from the Coinbase custodial wallet housed on the Coinbase exchange. So, if you trade on Coinbase but want to take more ownership of your crypto, you must transfer it to your Coinbase Wallet. You don't have to trade with Coinbase, or even have a Coinbase account, to use it.

The Coinbase Wallet keeps your cryptocurrencies safe with a self-custody design and the fact that it's separate from the Coinbase exchange. It has excellent security and offers the opportunity to trade a large number of tokens and NFTs, and it can be used to transact via Coinbase and other top decentralized exchanges. It also sports easier-to-remember, memorable wallet addresses (a unique set of characters that identify you as the owner and allow transactions to occur from your wallet). It's compatible with multiple cryptocurrencies including Bitcoin, Ethereum, Solana, Tronix, and others. It also supports all Ethereum Layer-2 platforms, but it doesn't support Bitcoin Cash or Ethereum Classic.

The Coinbase Wallet supports up to fifteen wallet addresses for both Ethereum and Solana, giving you the flexibility to create different wallets for different purposes. You can also import your existing Ethereum and Solana wallets to it or connect to Coinbase .com (or another exchange) and move assets from the wallet to the exchange and back. It also offers access to over one hundred dApps, which you can switch to with a single tap.

Coinbase Wallet isn't as user-friendly as other wallets, so it may not be the best one for beginners. It also doesn't feature live customer service, although it provides a knowledge database with information that may be useful when troubleshooting issues. However, you can connect the Coinbase app to a hardware wallet to keep your assets offline. The Coinbase app is free, but you may have to pay fees for any of the dApps with which you transact.

MetaMask
The MetaMask wallet is primarily useful for Ethereum blockchain related activities and ERC-20 tokens (ERC-20 is a set of rules and directives for making uniformly usable tokens on the Ethereum network). MetaMask is a free, open-source app and is available as a mobile app. To set up a MetaMask wallet, go to the website (https://metamask.io/download), download the appropriate app

for your browser or mobile device (Chrome, iOS, or other), and set up a password. Write it down and carefully store both the password and the secret recovery phrase (also called a seed phrase). Your information is encrypted in your browser. Once you download the app, the directions tell you how to set up the wallet.

MetaMask stores your information on its servers, so you can use it from any computer or phone. As with Binance Wallet, you can add multiple accounts to your MetaMask wallet in order to facilitate different types of transactions. You can't remove a Meta-Mask account, although you can remove accounts that you import to the wallet.

You can use MetaMask to deposit ether and related tokens to your account through Transak. Transak is a payment processing platform that lets you do crypto transactions through Metamask. You may also use an automated clearinghouse (or ACH, a traditional bank transfer option), which has a limit of $25,000 but may take days to be completed. It also charges a network fee depending on the transaction details.

Some Useful Tips for MetaMask

You can also send money and swap tokens via MetaMask. These transactions also have fees. You can transact with Ethereum dApps, such as Mintable, to create NFTs. Safety is important, so when you use MetaMask, make sure it's the only tab open on your browser and consider using a separate browser, exclusive to MetaMask. Also consider attaching a hardware wallet to your MetaMask wallet to store your cryptocurrency offline.

COLD WALLETS

Security First

Cold wallets are offline devices that let users store their private keys with less risk than hot wallets. They have online access via Wi-Fi, Bluetooth, and direct connection through USB ports via a common cable connection. Because they are offline, they require multiple additional steps to gain access to online transaction sites. The upside is that they are more secure because they are offline until users seek to gain online access.

Cold wallets usually have an evaluation assurance level (EAL) above 5. EAL is a measure of security; the higher the level, the more rigorous the security of a cold wallet. The inevitable disclaimer is that an EAL rating only guarantees that the device achieved the ascribed level of safety when it was tested in a specific place under a specific set of conditions.

LEDGER

The most popular cold wallet is Ledger, with the first generation called Ledger Nano S, a method of storing bitcoin offline. Since then, Ledger has produced other cold wallets and has expanded support for other crypto assets, including NFTs. Ledger wallets store private keys offline. When connected to smart devices, you can manage your crypto assets through Ledger Live (the software interface for the Ledger wallet) or patch into other wallets such as MetaMask and then conduct your transactions (like trading or staking).

You can recover access to your crypto assets in two ways. One is through a twenty-four-word recovery phrase. The other is to pay Ledger $9.99 per month to access Ledger Recover, which allows you to recover lost keys. Ledger Recover has been controversial, with some members of the community suggesting that it may decrease platform safety via weaknesses in code, which may make it vulnerable to hacks. There have been no reported incidents as of August 2025.

Types of Ledgers

The Ledger Nano S Plus, as are all Ledger wallets, is a hardware wallet. It sells for about $79 and has a 1.09-inch screen and a USB-C connection with an EAL rating of 6+. It offers access to multiple platforms through third-party wallets; however, it's only operational through a desktop computer or Android device.

The Ledger Nano X has a wider body but retains the 1.09-inch screen and sells for $149. Its battery allows for up to 5 hours of use. Its security rating is EAL 5+. It also has ANSSI CSPN certification (a high-level certification for safety issued by the French government).

The Ledger Stax is the most advanced Ledger device and retails for $399. It's equipped with a 3.7-inch curved screen and battery life of up to 10 hours or 150 transactions. It has a USB connection but also works through a Bluetooth connection and a near-field communication (NFC) capability. NFC is a slow, low-power connection activated between capable devices at a distance of 4 centimeters (approximately 1.5 inches). It's commonly used for no-contact mobile payments and similar endeavors.

TREZOR

Trezor is an open-source cold (hardware) wallet offering a double layer of security. The first line is via the seed phrase, common to all cold wallets. It also offers a passphrase that isn't stored to add to its inherent security.

Trezor launched its earliest model, the Trezor Model One, in 2014 and followed up with the Model T four years later. It currently offers three models:

- The Trezor Safe 5, released in 2024, is the most advanced Trezor yet. It sells for $169 and features a 1.54-inch Gorilla Glass (scratch-resistant) full-color touch screen. It has an EAL rating of 6+.
- The Trezor Safe 3 was released in October 2023. It costs $79 and comes with a 0.96-inch monochromatic screen and a two-button pad. The Trezor Safe 3 only has a USB-C connection.
- The Trezor Model One, the first Trezor model, was released in 2014. It costs $49 and has a 0.96-inch screen and a two-button pad. Its only connection mode is via a micro USB connection port.

Through the Trezor Suite app, users can connect their wallet to smart devices and perform transactions ranging from trading to paying bills. Trezor wallets offer several other attractive features. They support over a thousand coins and tokens, but do not support Solana or XRP. They can be integrated to work with multiple software wallets such as MetaMask. And aside from being inexpensive to purchase, they have built-in PIN and passphrase protection, along with advanced backup and recovery options.

SAFEPAL WALLETS

SafePal came on the scene in 2019 with its SafePal S1 wallet and since then, it has introduced two more models: the X1 and S1 Pro. SafePal wallets are compatible with over one hundred blockchain networks and a large number of NFTs and other tokens, which you can find by viewing the Safepal supported assets page (www.safepal.com/en/coin/lists). Each SafePal cold wallet app offers users safety and control of their crypto assets (it's Android, iOS, and desktop supported). The most attractive feature of the SafePal wallets is the built-in self-destruct mechanism, which erases all wallet data if the security mechanism of the wallet is tampered with (but don't worry, you can recover your wallet on a new SafePal device using your seed phrase).

The S1 and S1 Pro wallets sell for $49.99 and $89.99 respectively. The X1 sells for $69.99. Both the S1 and S1 Pro wallets are equipped with air-gapped signing mechanisms via QR codes, which means they do not rely on Internet or any other type of connection, thus increasing security. Both the S1 and S1 Pro have 1.3-inch full-color screens, while the X1 has a 1.8-inch monochrome screen and uses Bluetooth for signing in. All SafePal wallets have 5+ EAL ratings.

Pick Your Favorite

The three wallet platforms described in this section are representative of what's available in the cold wallet ecosystem. There are certainly other cold wallets in the market. Some are costlier—in the range of $400. Each individual wallet has its pros and cons, with their sign-in mechanisms and related security apparatus offering different variations. Users should take their time to research and choose one that meets their needs (whether it's affordability, security, or special needs such as platform interfaces, coin and token support, or ease of use).

MOBILE WALLETS

Hot Wallets for Your Mobile Phone

Mobile wallets are a specific type of hot wallet that run on mobile phone–based apps. Therefore, the basic operational tenets of hot wallets apply to mobile wallets. The key difference is that mobile wallets allow crypto users to manage their crypto assets on the go through their smartphones. Specifically, they allow storing, sending, and receiving cryptocurrencies to and from a smartphone. Their main advantage over other hot wallets is that they allow users to self-custody their cryptocurrencies, combined with the convenience of a smartphone app. Self-custody offers users control of their private keys. It's important to keep separate duplicates in case you forget them or something goes wrong with the wallet. When choosing a mobile app, it's important to prioritize security by safeguarding and backing up your private keys (it helps if the app has a built-in backup mechanism), as well as choosing an app with two-factor authentication.

Mobile wallets should not be confused with exchange/custodial wallets, as mobile wallets allow users to fully control their private keys and manage their assets directly and independently. On the other hand, exchange/custodial wallets are managed by a third party (the exchange), which holds the keys on behalf of the user.

There is a wide variety of mobile apps available. In many cases, they are versions of pre-existing hot or cold wallets on the market, or they're associated with major exchanges. Many have niche specific advantages, which offer users special advantages. This section focuses on what makes each mobile app specifically suitable for a given purpose.

Before choosing a mobile wallet, it's important to decide what you'll use it for, whether it's to store a single cryptocurrency or multiple. It also helps to know the ease of use, the safety record, and any other particulars related to each individual wallet, especially whether the wallet offers the opportunity for earning rewards through staking. If you choose this route, it's best to select the wallet that meets all of your needs. This section highlights two mobile wallets that offer an overview of the sector, which beginners can use as benchmarks.

TRUST WALLET

The Trust Wallet, which originated in 2017, is considered the best mobile wallet for beginners because of its ease of use. Acquired by Binance in 2018, Trust wallets can be used for storing, trading, and staking.

Trust Wallet is a free app supported on both the Android and iOS platforms with a simple downloading process. Its security is top-notch and includes biometric authentication and advanced encryption protection. Your private keys are stored on your device, ensuring only you have access to them. It also offers seamless interaction with the Ethereum platform while offering access to over four million cryptocurrency assets, sixty-five blockchains, staking, and NFT storing. It also offers an in-app exchange to facilitate swaps between different cryptocurrencies while also integrating easily with multiple popular dApps.

To earn rewards through staking with Trust as the platform, you select a coin from the group of supported cryptocurrencies on the app (such as Binance Coin) and choose a validator. Pick the one that offers the best rates and has the best reputation. Enter the amount you wish to stake, confirm the transaction, and start gathering rewards.

There are some small downsides to Trust: The user is responsible for safekeeping the password and seed phrase (if you lose them, your assets are lost) and there is no web-based access, as Trust exists only as a mobile app. And, because it's a mobile app, it may be less secure than a hardware wallet. For example, in November 2022, there was a security breach in Trust Wallet, which resulted in $170,000 in losses for users.

COINOMI WALLET

An alternative is Coinomi, a non-custodial mobile wallet with a large global following numbered in the millions. It was established in 2014 and is the oldest multichain wallet, meaning it's compatible with multiple blockchains. It offers both a desktop version (Windows, iOS, and Linux) and a mobile version of the app, which is supported in twenty-five languages.

Coinomi is often described as an "all-in-one" wallet because it offers its users a wide array of services, which increase the convenience of the app. As with all non-custodian wallets, it doesn't hold user keys on its servers. Instead, it stores them on your device, protected by encryption and your own set password. It offers a built-in exchange, which allows users to switch between coins inside the wallet without having to switch to another app. It also offers high-level security via two-factor authentication and seed phrase backup. In contrast to Trust, the seed phrase backup allows users to recover their coins if the wallet is lost.

Other features that set Coinomi apart from other wallets include its acceptance of over 1,700 cryptocurrencies, including bitcoin, ether, Solana, and Tronix, and that it offers access to over

120 blockchains. A further distinction is that Coinomi doesn't collect user data or sell it to third parties.

Coinomi offers users rewards via a cold staking mechanism, where the user keeps the staked coins offline and increases the security of the holdings by keeping them offline. By keeping the staked holdings offline, users gain passive income and retain the ownership and control of their assets.

One limitation is that Coinomi does not support NFT storage. This means that if you own a unique digital asset, artwork or otherwise, you can't store it in Coinomi. A viable alternative is Meta-Mask. Another criticism of Coinomi is that it's not completely open source—the app's code can't be vetted for safety by outsiders.

In the crypto community, that translates to "nontransparency," which limits an individual user's ability to verify the safety of the app because no one but the company can verify that the underlying code is safe. At the very least, it engenders mistrust on the part of some in the user community, as it's seen as a potential vulnerability in the code.

Coinomi claims its wallet has never been hacked, but there is a controversial report that claims a $60,000 breach occurred in 2019, which fuels the "open source" controversy about the app. The company denied the issue, describing it as a technical glitch that involved Google and did not result in any losses, as Google never validated the transaction.

Focus on Safety

It's important to remember that both hot wallets and mobile wallets are always connected to the Internet, meaning that there is a risk of being hacked. So, you might consider adding extra protection to your mobile devices, such as a virtual private network (VPN).

CRYPTOCURRENCY AS PAYMENTS

Growth in Worldwide Usage

As of 2025, about 6.8% of the total world population (more than 560 million people) own crypto, while some reviews suggest that as many as 46% of businesses accept crypto as part of their payment systems. The countries with the largest crypto ownership are India, Nigeria, Indonesia, and the US.

Certainly, India's large population is a boost to the crypto world. Yet, the GENIUS Act and the US government's embracing of crypto as a viable (albeit dollar-backed) currency is helping to smooth out the transitional bumps from fiat currencies to cryptocurrencies. It could certainly take time for the full, or nearly full, acceptance of crypto as a dominant form of currency in the world. While cryptocurrencies are steadily gaining in acceptance as both investments and a method of transferring value, the logical progression beyond ownership is the use of crypto as spending money.

CRYPTO DEMOGRAPHICS AND EMERGING TRENDS

Rigorous regulation is needed in order to fully incorporate cryptocurrency into the financial system. That's because there are so many moving parts, ranging from the expansion of investing vehicles for crypto to its widening acceptance via major financial firms (Mastercard and PayPal), major banks (JPMorgan Chase), and diverse retailers and businesses (Apple, Microsoft, and Home

Depot). Another significant factor in the increased accessibility and use of crypto is the rise in stablecoins (cryptocurrencies that are pegged to fiat currencies such as the US dollar and hard assets such as gold, thus making them less volatile in their price).

Additionally, lower transaction fees, especially for international transactions, are increasing the acceptance of cryptocurrencies as a valid method of exchange. Another positive trend is the rapid development of government regulations to address the risk of fraud in the system.

Yet, with about 6.8% of the world's population owning cryptocur-rencies, it's important to know which segments of the population are actually using crypto for payments today. Young adults (between the ages of twenty-five and thirty-four), tech savvy consumers who value decentralization, and higher income individuals are the most frequent users of crypto as a mode of payment. Moreover, frequent online consumers are flocking to crypto and are willing to flock to businesses who accept crypto as payment. There is also an emerging subeconomy based on crypto in emerging countries and an increase in the use of crypto debit and credit cards.

Advantages of Using Crypto As Payments

The major advantage of using crypto as a payment method is that it centralizes your money in a single place (your wallet) and gives you complete control of where and when it goes while offering privacy and anonymity. The major disadvantage is that any time you pay with crypto, you are potentially creating a complex tax event.

HOW TO MAKE PAYMENTS WITH CRYPTO

You can make payments with crypto by following a few simple steps. Be aware that different apps or wallets can operate differently from others. Here are some basic steps to get you started:

1. Choose a Web3 username. This is similar to an Internet domain, and it simplifies the process because you don't have to type your lengthy and complicated wallet address, which may have over thirty numbers and letters. A Web3 username is much smaller and can be as simple as typing your name and your chosen domain name.
2. Set up a wallet. This is part of the process when you open your crypto account; simply follow the steps when prompted.
3. Acquire some cryptocurrency and store it in your chosen wallet (inside an exchange or offline depending on your risk tolerance, your experience, and a review of the fees involved in each potential wallet).
4. Send payments. Open your wallet app, click on the "Send Payment" button, and enter the amount you want to send. Enter the QR code or wallet address of the recipient.
5. Click the "Send" button.

    To receive payments:

1. Open your wallet app.
2. Click the "Receive Payment" button.
3. Share your public key (never your private key) with the sender.
4. Accept the payment when it appears in your wallet.

RISKS WHEN MAKING
OR RECEIVING PAYMENTS

Be aware that there are risks involved when making or accepting payments with crypto. The most important one is that crypto transactions are irreversible. If you buy something but then decide you want a refund, there may be some difficulties and delays depending on who you did the transaction with. It may be that the only way you get your money back is that the counterparty is willing to return it.

The second most important aspect of crypto transactions is that, depending on the transaction type, there may be a tax liability that you're not aware of. That's because the IRS considers crypto as property. So, any transaction could be a gain or a loss depending on the value of the cryptocurrency on the day of the transaction. This means immaculate recordkeeping is crucial, including knowing the value of the crypto you accept on the day of the transaction.

Finally, if you lose your private keys, you may lose access to your wallet unless you've chosen a wallet with a key backup mechanism. This can create significant problems, as the crypto you're holding in the wallet can fall in value from the time you lose the key to the time you retrieve it (if you're fortunate enough to recover it).

CRYPTO STAKING

A Way to Monetize Your Crypto Assets

Staking is the practice of locking up your tokens in a specialized wallet held in a blockchain to provide security and support the operation of the blockchain. Staking takes place in proof of stake (PoS) blockchains such as Ethereum, Cardano, and Solana. When you stake your holdings, you receive rewards (usually in the form of blockchain tokens). The rewards can provide a stream of income, which over time could increase your crypto holdings.

When you lock up your tokens, you're setting them aside for the use of the blockchain. This means you can't trade, lend, or withdraw them. The longer you lock up your tokens, the larger the rewards. Staking can be a win-win, as it provides users with income and benefits the blockchain by providing liquidity, validating transactions, and securing the blockchain.

Staking was first introduced in 2012 after a paper proposing the practice was published. Peercoin was the first cryptocurrency to implement staking. When Ethereum switched from a proof of work (PoW) to a PoS blockchain in 2022, it increased the cryptocurrency world's interest in staking. As of 2025, staking continues to grow as a way for crypto users to derive income from their holdings while also providing benefits to the blockchain.

STAKING SIMPLIFIED

Assume blockchain X is offering a 10% return for your staked tokens for a one-month staking period. You decide to offer them

100 tokens for lockup. In this arrangement, in a month, blockchain X would return your original tokens plus an additional 10 tokens.

To stake your tokens, follow these five simple steps:

1. Choose a cryptocurrency that allows staking.
2. Acquire the cryptocurrency.
3. Decide what type of staking you'll engage in (details in the following section) and what type of platform you'll be doing your staking business with.
4. Stake your cryptocurrency by following the terms of the platform or method you've decided to go with.
5. Earn rewards.

So, while it's easy on paper, it still requires some forethought before you begin staking your crypto.

TYPES OF STAKING

There are several methods of staking. On a macro level, these methods can be summed up in two categories: custodial staking, where a custodian (such as an exchange) holds the locked-up tokens, and non-custodial staking, which allows you to hold the staked tokens in your own wallet.

In custodial staking (also known as passive staking), the custodian manages the staking process. This ensures that the process is handled appropriately. You retain control of your assets, but the custodian controls the staking operation. As a result, the custodian takes a portion of the rewards. A standard custodian arrangement means that the custodian stakes your assets and does not use them for any other purpose.

Non-custodial staking is also known as active staking. There are several ways to actively stake tokens, which include the following:

- **Solo staking:** This is where you set up your own node (computer dedicated to crypto) and manage the entire process. Solo staking requires a great deal of expertise and expense.
- **Staking as a service:** In this method, you delegate the staking process to a third party and pay them a fee for managing your node. You still control your assets; however, you will have to split fees with the third party. Because there is risk involved, you should thoroughly research any third party before engaging with them for business.
- **Delegated staking:** When you use delegated staking, you allow a third party to stake your tokens but you retain ownership. This staking method lets you reap rewards while allowing an experienced third party to make the staking decisions.
- **Pooled staking:** A group of crypto users pool their resources to stake together. Pooled staking increases the chances of being chosen as a validator and increases the earnings potential of a staking venture.

Staking offers a way to gain rewards with a different risk profile than trading crypto. Before jumping in, however, make sure you have all the pertinent details.

THE CURRENT STATUS OF STAKING

In 2025, the SEC updated the guidelines for staking and clarified the legalities. Their decision to define solo and delegated staking as *not* security offerings was particularly useful. This decision cleared the way for larger participation in staking. Specifically, the SEC stated that solo staking, delegated staking, and custodial staking are legal and comply with US securities laws. The SEC deemed that yield farming (schemes that promise specific guaranteed returns) and staking-disguised lending (any staking that resembles lending) are not allowed.

Cryptocurrencies that provide the best returns for staking include BNB, ATOM, Polkadot, CRO, ALGO, and Ethereum. The potential returns (real rewards), in a sampled 2025 snapshot, ranged from Ether (4.1%) to Binance Coin (7.43%).

SOME NUANCES TO CONSIDER

The allure of staking is that you earn rewards from your crypto holdings with less risk than you might encounter with trading. But there are some drawbacks to consider as well. Specifically, there are no guarantees that you will receive your rewards. Certain developments, aside from fraud, can gum up the works. For example, with network congestion, the most likely outcome is a slow delivery of your rewards. Network congestion is caused by the number of active transactions exceeding a network's capacity to process transactions. It also increases network fees. Congestion can result from several events such as external situations increasing volume, a sudden increase in price volatility, an increase in complex transactions, or the launch of new tokens. Another delay with receiving rewards may happen if you have bad luck with your validator being dishonest or error-prone. Or, finally, you may have issues if there's a change in the blockchain protocol, such as a fork, where a new version of the blockchain emerges.

Chapter 5

Mining Cryptocurrency

Cryptocurrency mining is the process through which certain new coins are minted and how transactions are processed and recorded. Crypto mining is a nuanced, digital version of traditional mineral mining and has a similar process (in principle) to gold mining. Just like digging for gold, crypto mining is a rigorous and energy-consuming process.

Specifically, crypto mining is accomplished through high performance computing (HPC), a type of technology that uses powerful computer systems to solve complex equations, whose solutions lead to the minting of new tokens and the validation and recording of transactions in a proof of work (PoW) blockchain. The basic measure of how fast a coin is minted or a transaction is processed is the hash rate; "hashing" is the process through which informational inputs are transformed into a specific and unique data fingerprint, which ensures the security and authenticity of the cryptocurrency transaction it is recording. Hashes prove the validity of the event (transaction/token creation).

Theoretically, anyone can be a crypto miner. In reality, because of the requirements of HPC, crypto mining has become realistic for companies with enough resources to carry out the task efficiently and securely. This chapter is all about the intricacies of crypto mining, ranging from mining gear to the many types of mining out there.

FUNDAMENTALS OF MINING

Learn How It's Done

To fully understand mining, a brief history of the process and the computers involved is helpful. The first Bitcoin block was mined in 2009 by Satoshi Nakamoto. Mining began with the traditional method of computing based on the central processing unit (CPU) model—the operational circuits of traditional computing. The CPU model proved too slow; thus, miners transitioned to the graphics processing unit (GPU) model. GPUs are a more efficient set of circuits originally used in gaming, allowing computers to do more work at a faster pace in AI- and cryptocurrency-related transactions.

Field-programmable gate arrays (FPGAs) were introduced in 1985. These are initially generic semiconductors that are programmable for site-specific operations. They can be put into service more rapidly, can be programmed for specific tasks, and reprogrammed for different operations. Application-specific integrated circuits (ASICs), have been around since the 1960s, but emerged as crucial cogs in the crypto machine in 2013. They're smaller in size and offer a higher level of performance with lower power consumption.

HOW CRYPTOCURRENCY MINING WORKS

Here's a breakdown of what happens behind the scenes when a user initiates a transaction (trading, staking, transferring, or making a purchase) with crypto. There are seven steps involved in cryptocurrency mining. Each is inherently important in the smooth function of the blockchain:

- **Before completion, transactions are pooled.** When crypto transactions are initiated, they are grouped into a pool. Each transaction contains information about the transaction and a transaction fee. Pooling reduces the cost of transactions.
- **Uncompleted transactions are combined into a block.** Large transactions, those with the potential for larger processing fees, or transactions that have been waiting the longest may be prioritized.
- **Miners compete to solve the transactional puzzle.** Once a block is assembled, miners race to solve the equation that will lead to the nonce, a number that produces a hash when combined with the block's data.
- **The fastest miner to solve the puzzle creates a valid hash.** They inform the blockchain that the puzzle is solved, triggering the next step in the chain.
- **Other miners then verify the solution to the puzzle.** When enough miners agree on the solution, a consensus is reached based on the rules of the blockchain protocol.
- **The first miner to broadcast the solution then processes the transaction.** This results in a new block added to the blockchain and confirms all the transactions in the block to the blockchain. New tokens are then added to the blockchain depending on the rules of the blockchain.
- **The miner who solved the puzzle receives a reward.** This can be in the form of payment and/or tokens depending on the rules of the blockchain. If you process a block on Bitcoin,

your payment is in bitcoin. If on the Ethereum blockchain, your payment is in Ether. The successful miner can keep the reward, trade it, or exchange it for dollars/other fiat currencies.

MINED VERSUS NON-MINED COINS

Because of the size and importance of the crypto market's presence in the financial system, it's important to know the difference between mined and non-mined coins. In general, mined coins operate under the proof of work (PoW) protocol, the process through which crypto miners solve complex mathematical equations to validate transactions. All mined coins operate under the PoW protocol. Non-mined coins, on the other hand, operate under the proof of stake (PoS) protocol. PoS is the process through which blockchain validators are allowed to validate transactions based on the amount of cryptocurrency they own and are willing to stake.

Non-mined (pre-mined) coins fall into two categories. One category features any coins where their full supply has been released to the public after they have been "pre-mined" (created) by the developer; their numbers are limited. An example of a pre-mined coin is ADA. The other subset are the coins where the entire supply is not in circulation. Their supply can only grow through other methods such as wallet staking or master node creation. Master nodes are specialized servers that perform traditional crypto transactions such as validating, but also perform specific functions including making transactions anonymous, clearing transactions, and participating in blockchain governance.

As of this writing, popular mined coins include bitcoin (BTC), Monero (XMR), Litecoin (LTC), Ethereum Classic (ETC), Dogecoin

(DOGE), and Zcash (ZEC). The most popular member of the group is bitcoin because of its market dominance and the higher rewards it pays for mining. For example, a successful Bitcoin mining exercise may deliver 3.125 BTC as a reward (over $300,000 based on August 2025 pricing). In comparison, a successful mining of Dogecoin may pay 10,000 DOGE tokens (approximately $2,300).

A Coin's Real Purpose

Whether a coin is mined or not, its major function is to validate transactions. Aside from their practical functions as a storage of value, investment vehicles, and methods of standardized value transfer, cryptocurrencies achieve network consensus of the validity of a transaction. This process prevents an event (transaction) from occurring more than once. Because cryptocurrencies were designed to decentralize finance (taking out the middleman: banks), validation of transactions is required to keep the blockchain functional.

SOME MINING SPECIFICS

The granular details of mining are worth mentioning. Essentially, the processor (CPU, GPU, or ASIC) grinds (creates hashes) to find the solution to the cryptographic puzzle, which is finished when it finds a value equal to or less than the target difficulty's intended value—the answer to the puzzle. Once the puzzle is solved, it must be verified by the blockchain. This is a highly competitive process that leads to rewards for the winning computer.

REASONS FOR AND AGAINST MINING CRYPTOCURRENCY

The Good, the Bad, and the Rest of It

The process of crypto mining is designed to provide security for the blockchain through PoW. The inherent feature of this security is meant to prevent a single individual or a coordinated group from obtaining 50% control of the blockchain. Mining requires a great deal of computing power and, through mining, blockchain integrity is virtually guaranteed because of the extreme amount of HPC that would be required to control 50% of the blockchain.

Non-mineable coins are nuanced in their own ways. For example, a major reason for non-mineable coins is that the entire supply of coins is "pre-mined" by the developers, and the entire supply is then made available, partially or fully, to the public. Partial releases are often because the developer wants to keep some coins to finance the project.

CRYPTO MINING PROS AND CONS

The benefits of crypto mining are based around the security, decentralization of the system, and potential for greater rewards. Additionally, the decentralized nature of the process theoretically offers anyone access to the mining process and its potential rewards. However, the combination of the energy required to mine coins, the increasingly specialized hardware, and the likelihood of decreased profits due to the combination of those factors, reduces the potential for the public's participation in coin mining. The mining process has now morphed into a corporate endeavor. That said, investors can now participate in the profit potential of mining through publicly traded companies specializing in the process.

While mineable coins are created through the rigorous process of mining—a decentralized process involving competition—non-mineable coins are produced by a less energy-consuming process. In other words, non-mineable coins offer the advantage of requiring less energy consumption and less capital investment for the retail user of cryptocurrency. Thus, instead of spending large sums of money on HPC equipment, the real estate to house it, and the expense of the energy required to operate the system, you can just set up a wallet and conduct crypto-related transactions for non-mineable coins.

There are crypto enthusiasts who balk at non-mined coins, describing the system as "less fair" than mined coins. They think that because the coins are pre-mined, access is more centralized and controlled by the coin's developers. The most "sticky" point is that the developers often keep a significant portion of the coins for personal or blockchain-related use. Plus, the PoS protocol is often seen as less safe than the more established PoW system.

Indeed, there is a tendency for users to trust PoS (non-mined coins) platforms less than PoW platforms (mined coins) due to the perception that there is a higher chance of fraud in the former.

THE RUG PULL

A specific type of fraud inherent to cryptocurrencies is known as the "rug pull." That's where a developer of a new token or NFT "hypes up" a project in order to attract investors and then suddenly shuts down the project, taking the money and disappearing.

There are two types of rug pulls: hard and soft. A hard rug pull is an intentional scam where the "developer" has no intention of completing the project or releasing the token. The goal is to steal money and disappear. This is often accomplished by "hardwiring" the investment process by designing the tokens to allow for theft. A soft rug pull is where theft occurs slowly and the investor gets a false sense of security. As the name implies, this is a subtle con designed to be deployed on unsuspecting victims over time. This is usually accomplished by the founders of the new token dumping their tokens in the early stages of the unveiling of the blockchain, while still pretending to be actively involved. By the time the scam unravels, usually when the founders abandon the project, the perpetrators' stakes have been liquidated; they are long gone, and the investors are left holding the bag.

More specific details of rug pulls include:

- **Dumping** is when the developer offers large rewards for participation in the token's fortunes to drive up the price of the token. At some point, the developer sells its own supply, which causes the price of the token to plummet, and leaves the scene as investors face the losses.
- **Liquidity stealing** is conducted via loopholes built into the smart contracts required for the token's participation in the blockchain. These loopholes allow for the developer's stealing of tokens from investors.
- **Limiting sell orders** is a scheme that involves the developer permitting unlimited buying of tokens but restricts or doesn't allow the sale of the token by the public. The developer,

meanwhile, dumps their own tokens, which causes the price to plummet, leaving investors stuck with worthless tokens.

All types of rug pulls are done with bad intent, making mining possibly (financially) dangerous for any level of investor.

SAFETY TIPS

Because of the potential for fraud in crypto, especially in non-mined coins, there are important safeguards to implement. When considering investing in a new token, thoroughly research the development team. Pay close attention to the project's intentions, goals, how they distribute information, and whether it's truthful and verifiable. Be especially careful of unrealistic return promises. For example, if you know that you can receive a verifiable 5% return by staking your Ethereum tokens, and a new XYZ token promises a 20% return, that's a reason to avoid the new token. A surefire way to avoid fraud is to engage with the community. If something's fishy, it will come out in chats and other communications.

Mining Today

Mining is a highly competitive industry that requires specialized hardware and substantial electricity. The mining process is essential for maintaining the integrity of the blockchain and ensuring the security of transactions. As of August 2025, Bitcoin mining rewards are 6.25 BTC per block, with a new block mined approximately every 10 minutes.

BASICS OF MINING GEAR

What You Need to Mine Cryptocurrencies

Cryptocurrency mining can provide passive income; however, it can be an expensive endeavor that requires planning, budgeting, and a thorough review of local regulations for any setup requirements, especially those related to power consumption that apply in your area. Depending on your setup, you may also be limited to which coins you can mine, as the technology required may be beyond a home computer; even the most commonly used home "rigs" for mining, such as gaming setups, may not be sufficient. For example, Bitcoin mining is reserved for sophisticated HPC-ASIC enabled setups.

Alternative coins that are still mineable through home mining rigs (the computer setup through which you will conduct your mining endeavors) include Ethereum Classic (ETC), Ravencoin (RVN), Zcash (ZEC), and Dogecoin (DOGE). These coins are mineable via a GPU-powered rig.

The basic setup includes a CPU- or GPU-powered computer. GPU is preferrable, with at least the most powerful gaming setup advisable, though a specially built rig with multiple GPUs is optimal. Other requirements include a well-ventilated place for your rig, a reliable power supply, a cooling system, a secure crypto wallet, and a stout and highly reliable Internet connection.

Your rig's setup should include enough room for the computing, cooling, and power supply equipment. It should also be a place where the electricity supply and Internet access is both available and reliable. Typical places include basements, garages, spare rooms, and storage areas. Also, make sure to check each location for water leaks (or other related issues) and ensure that your locality allows for home-based crypto mining rigs. Given that an adequate GPU-based rig may require six GPUs, your baseline cost is anywhere from $2,400 to $10,000 or more, not including the rest of your setup.

REQUIRED COMPUTING HARDWARE

The computer system for your home mining rig should include a powerful GPU (8–24 gigabytes (GB)—higher is better, though the cost may be over $3,000); a motherboard with multiple Peripheral Component Interconnect Express (PCIe) slots, which connects different hardware components such as graphics and sound cards, allowing them to communicate and operate at maximum speed and efficiency; a stout power supply unit (PSU); and sufficient random access memory, or RAM (4–8 GB) and storage memory (50 GB hard drive). These are the starting parameters, and costs should be carefully considered.

THE POWER SUPPLY UNIT

The hardest working component of your mining rig is PSU, which converts wall outlet alternating current (AC) to direct current (DC); this is required to run GPU and ASICs machines. DC is more efficient and reliable than AC for tasks such as mining. For a home GPU-based setup, you can choose advanced technology extended (ATX) PSUs (traditional power supply units) to power your rig. A server PSU may work if your setup is suited for it. PSUs that have 20%–30% more capacity than your rig requirements are optimal, as they keep the system stable and efficient while preventing overload. Use PSUs with 80 PLUS Gold, Platinum, or Titanium certification. Make sure your computer PSU connectors match.

COOLING SYSTEMS

A cooling system is necessary as your rig will be on 24/7 and will produce a lot of heat. There are three types of cooling systems: air, immersion cooling, and hydro cooling systems.

The most commonly used system is air via the combined use of a well-ventilated room filled with strategically placed fans near the rig. This is the most inexpensive and easy to implement. The limitations are required frequent cleaning for dust and the potential for its being ineffective during periods of high outside temperatures.

An immersion cooling system requires placing your mining rig in a nonconductive liquid such as synthetic hydrocarbons, esters, and fluorochemicals. You can even use mineral oil. They all absorb heat and do not conduct electricity. The limiting factors are the cost (hydrocarbons, esters, and fluorochemicals tend to be more expensive) and their effectiveness. There is always the potential for spills and toxicity. Make sure the liquid you choose is compatible with your mining rig (hardware).

A hydro cooling system is water-based, and it's composed of racks, coolant pumps, filtration system, heat exchangers, a control system, and PSUs. Hydro cooling systems are more efficient than air cooling systems, can take up less room, and may be less noisy to operate. They may be more expensive and require professional expertise to install and maintain. Over time, they may extend the life of your rig, neutralizing the initial investment.

MINING SOFTWARE

A crypto mining software program allows your computer to solve the equations required to mine cryptocurrencies. These specialized programs connect your crypto mining rig to blockchain platforms and allow your mining interactions to take place. There are two types of software: general and specific. General mining software can function with several coins, while specific programs function with single coins.

Types of Mining Software

- CudoMiner is a type of software supporting multiple currencies. Its features include automated coin switching, which means the software automatically switches your account to the coin that is offering the best conditions in the current market, and remote management, so users can monitor and control their mining while on the go. It functions on CPU, GPU, and ASICs machines.
- EasyMiner also supports multiple currencies, is user-friendly, and supports solo and pool mining. It works on CPU and GPU rigs.
- XMRig is best suited for Monero and operates on both CPU and GPU computers.

Regardless of what your setup looks like, these basics will ensure that your setup has the best chance of success.

CLOUD MINING

Easier for Beginner Miners

Cloud mining is a worthwhile, passive income–generating alternative to running your own home-based crypto mining operation. This is especially attractive for a beginner, though the start-up costs should be carefully weighed before jumping in. That said, cloud mining is attractive because it doesn't require the dedication of a room in your home for crypto mining, thus reducing the risk of major issues developing in your house, such as an increase in your electricity bill, the potential for fires (due to rig overheating), or flooding (if your cooling system malfunctions).

Cloud mining is the practice of crypto mining off-site via the rental of computer power and equipment from a crypto mining data center. You reap rewards based on the size of your rental. The main advantages are reduced cost (compared to setting up your own crypto mining operation) and an increasing chance of receiving rewards (since you're part of a mining pool). The major disadvantages are that, unless you choose the proper "landlord," you may be scammed and the rewards may not be very big.

When you decide to cloud mine, you can choose from a variety of potential arrangements. A simple approach is to rent a certain amount of "hash power," a portion of the available mining capacity of a crypto mining data center. In some cloud mining arrangements, your power rental may be combined with the "hash power" rented by other miners in a mining pool. This pooling increases the odds of success in mining new blocks and gaining rewards. When the mining pool successfully mines a coin, the proceeds are distributed based on how much mining power each participant holds. Hash power mining is convenient since you don't have to buy equipment. However, this arrangement is prone to scams if you contract with a dishonest host, so stick to Binance or other major hosts.

Cloud mining costs depend on how much power, space, and equipment you rent and for how long. Depending on the contract, the cost may be from $25–$50 or more with time ranges anywhere from one day to twelve months. Other costs may include pass-through electricity and maintenance fees. Much depends on which platform you use and the contracted details of your arrangement. Binance, Hashmart, and ECOS offer Bitcoin cloud mining arrangements where all you buy is the hash power.

OTHER TYPES OF CLOUD MINING

There are other types of cloud mining approaches, like host mining. This is a completely hands-off endeavor where the host provides the entire infrastructure package (mining hardware, space to operate it, power and maintenance) and charges you a fee for the use of the setup. The host provides a safe premise for your rented rig (behind climate-controlled, closed doors with reliable electricity, 24/7 video surveillance, and remote monitoring capabilities). This type of arrangement is often suitable for beginners or those who prefer a hands-off approach. A slightly different approach to host mining, is the Bring Your Own Miner (BYOM) arrangement in which you own your rig and rent the space in which it will operate from the host. Either way, through host mining or BYOM, you can mine cryptocurrencies without managing the technical issues such as choosing hardware and having to sort through all the costs.

You still pay the host a rental and maintenance fee, and the host will also pass electricity costs to you. This makes sense if you're not interested in creating a suitable holding place in your home for your rig and to own and maintain the necessary equipment to keep it operational. It's important to understand that in both host mining and BYOM arrangements, you're responsible for deciding which coins to mine and when to mine them.

BYOM may also be suitable for more experienced miners, especially those who have ASIC rigs, which require a different level of set up and maintenance compared to GPU rigs. Certainly, there are hosts for both GPU and ASIC rigs. Whatever you do, there are different costs, depending on your requirements, both up-front, and with related maintenance and electricity.

There are many ways to set up a cloud mining operation with varying levels of responsibility and expense. Still, rental, maintenance, and electricity costs exist. So, you must evaluate whether the costs are low enough for you to run a profitable mining business.

Locations to Mine

Places that may be suitable for cloud mining include Las Vegas, where electricity costs can be attractive (lots of sunshine to power solar electricity) and the regulatory environment is favorable. North Carolina may be worth exploring as well, given its welcoming business climate and attractive zoning laws. The Research Triangle, located in the Piedmont region in North Carolina (Raleigh, Durham, and Chapel Hill) is known for its attractive location for hosting services. Finally, parts of Texas (Rockdale) or North Dakota (Williston, Bismark, Grand Forks) are also worth researching.

CPU MINING

Another Great Place to Start

CPU mining is a great place to start your mining enterprise because it's relatively low-tech and may be less expensive. It can be done with a regular computer, without the expensive equipment used in GPU or ASIC mining. CPU mining has been around since the early days of crypto and is still widely used. The CPU of your computer is the centerpiece of this mining process, which is combined with mining software that solves the mathematical puzzles that lead to coins and rewards. However, the rewards are likely to be smaller compared to rewards earned from GPU or ASIC mining rigs.

CPU mining can be taxing on your laptop, so you may consider buying a separate unit, perhaps with an advanced processor, and dedicating it solely to mining. A good place to start is with a decent-level gaming system. As with other mining methods, CPU mining may generate a great amount of heat, so plan accordingly.

Consider mining less popular altcoins since Bitcoin's mining space is highly competitive and usually requires GPU or ASIC rigs to deliver adequate rewards. Here are some alternative CPU mining compatible coins: Monero (XMR), Bytecoin (BCN), Electroneum (ETN), Aeon (AEON), Sumokoin (SUMO), Karbo (KRB), DigitalNote (XDN), TurtleCoin (TRTL), and Graft (GRFT). Each have their pros and cons for you to research.

GETTING STARTED WITH HARDWARE AND SOFTWARE

Setting up your CPU mining rig isn't much different than setting up a more complex GPU or ASIC operation. You still need computing power, software, and support systems to make the system operate optimally.

Hardware Requirements

Your hardware can range from a laptop to a fully tricked-out gaming rig. Your choice depends on your budget and expectations for rewards (the income that your mining endeavor will generate). Generally speaking, your CPU should be either an Intel or Advanced Micro Devices (AMD) chip, as these are reliable and well-made units. The Intel Core i5, i7, and i9 series, as well as the AMD Ryzen series, are suitable for CPU mining.

You can invest in more or less expensive models based on your budget and expectations. A simple model is to calculate how much "hash rate" a CPU will generate based on its cost. You can calculate this via a CPU mining profitability calculator such as the one offered by CryptoCompare (www.cryptocompare.com/mining/calculator), which lets you see the amount of power required to mine a coin based on the price of the coin you plug into the calculator. After you plug in all the parameters, the calculator will compute the potential profit of mining a coin based on your inputs. Here are some useful guidelines:

- Use the highest possible CPU and consider a Linux operating system, as they tend to mine better than Windows systems.

- Use the best possible power supply and cooling systems you can afford.
- Monitor your electricity costs and monitor your rig regularly.
- Be aware of the current mining conditions, especially the market price of the coins, how much mining competition is currently active in the market, and whether your operation is profitable.
- Consider diversifying into mining multiple coins.

By sticking to these guidelines, you should have a fair idea of how your setup will perform.

Software Requirements

The first step is to download software that is compatible with the coin(s) you intend to mine through your CPU rig. Look for apps that are user-friendly and have low crash rates and reliable functionality, while providing high hash rates. The hash rate is the speed at which a blockchain performs the hash calculations required for validation of transactions and adding new blocks to the chain. The higher the hash rate, the better odds of mining success. In addition, seek secure apps that include two-factor authentication and offer frequent security updates and an active support community. There are several free programs that are compatible with laptops and desktop computers:

- **EasyMiner** is highly recommended for beginners because of its user-friendly interface and its support for multiple cryptocurrencies.
- **MultiMiner** is compatible with CPU and GPU systems. With this software, you can switch between different mining algorithms.
- **CudoMiner** is designed to magnify profits through automation and lets you grow your mining craft without switching programs.

You should research the details of each program before installing it and be ready to switch if it doesn't meet your expectations. Always beware of potential scams.

Final Steps

Once you've got your hardware, software, wallet, and support systems in place, make sure you know the legal and regulatory rules with mining in your local region. Also consider joining a mining pool to increase your chances of profitability. Always remain flexible regarding your equipment and the coins you're trying to mine.

GPU MINING

The Next Step

GPU mining was introduced in 2010 and gathered momentum during the 2013–2017 boom in crypto. Mining is accomplished by the computer's processing one hash at a time: a simple and repetitive task. GPU mining is faster, more efficient, and is able to process more transactions than CPU mining, therefore excelling at the repetitive process of mining. However, since the advent of ASIC processors, it's not as prevalent or profitable as it once was. Still, it's a viable alternative, assuming you understand the risk-benefit ratio between costs and the potential for profitability.

ABOUT GPUS

GPUs are used to solve the complex equations needed to mine coins and potentially earn rewards. Because they have multiple cores (processing units) in a single circuit, they are able to conduct a larger number of operations at a faster speed than CPUs. CPUs have generally four to sixteen cores, while GPUs have hundreds to thousands of cores. CPUs are designed for sequential processing (one task follows another task upon the initial task's completion), while GPUs process smaller tasks simultaneously, making them more suitable for crypto mining.

Issues with Mining

China banned all crypto mining in 2021, citing environmental concerns. The shift toward proof of stake (PoS) protocols in blockchains such as Ethereum has also affected the use of GPUs in crypto mining.

PROS AND CONS OF GPU MINING

GPU mining makes sense as long as it fits your chosen parameters for success. It's important to consider the following before starting a GPU mining operation:

- Although GPUs cost more up front than CPUs, they have a higher hash rate. Thus, they can mine more coins in shorter periods of time. They are also more energy efficient, which may reduce your electrical bills, have less negative impacts on the environment, and further increase your profitability.
- They have larger memory capacity than CPUs, including short-term memory (cache), which means they store frequently used data and can access it rapidly without having to be issued instructions for the same task over and over.
- GPUs may offer the ability to mine a wider variety of coins.
- Maintenance and repair costs may be higher than those for a CPU rig.

Assessing these ideas is important before running out to get your hands on an upgraded GPU.

PROCESSING THE INS AND OUTS OF A GPU RIG

Unless you know your way around computers, building a GPU rig is best left to the experts, which, of course, adds cost to your setup. Most experts will recommend using Nvidia or AMD GPU arrays; the Nvidia GeForce RTX 5080 and GeForce RTX 3060 models have received good reviews based on price and performance. Both of these arrays combine all the attractive features described previously related to memory, speed, and power consumption, while offering a reasonable time period in which they may return your initial investment.

The RTX 3060 costs less and may be more suitable as an entry point. It has lower memory and performance standards, but its lower price compensates well for the difference. It can be used for both gaming and mining, while offering lower power requirements.

The fastest Nvidia GPU is the GeForce RTX 5090, part of its groundbreaking Blackwell series. It has the largest memory and processing speed of all its GPUs but may run a price tag of $2,000 or more.

The AMD Radeon RX 7900 XTX is considered a viable alternative GPU to the Nvidia options. It can be less expensive and may be more widely available, but it is generally considered to be AMD's most expensive GPU processor.

THE REALITY CHECK

GPU mining is a viable option, but it's facing significant competition from ASICs-driven mining, especially in Bitcoin. Moreover, Ether, one of the most mining-intensive coins that made excellent use of GPUs (and featured an ASICs-resistant algorithm), has moved to a PoS platform, and it has somewhat diminished the appeal for GPU mining. You can still mine Ethereum Classic through your GPU rig. Remember: There is intense competition in cryptocurrency mining; large corporate players with massive server capacity housed in huge data centers have a distinct advantage over home-based miners.

Getting a GPU Processor

GPU prices can shift rapidly. You can buy GPU processors at Amazon.com or Walmart.com. The downside, and the reason for the potential price shifts, is that supplies may be tight depending on demand, which can be based on the status of the crypto market at any time. During some periods, the asking price for a GPU may be above the manufacturer's suggested retail price (MSRP). You can counter supply issues by considering a used GPU unit.

ASIC MINING

The Latest and Greatest . . . So Far

Application-specific integrated circuits (ASIC) miners originated in 2012 and have revolutionized the crypto mining ecosystem. ASICs have one function: to mine cryptocurrencies (especially bitcoin). As a result, they are faster and more efficient than CPUs and GPUs. How much faster? An ASICs processor can generate (hash) more than 400 terahashes per second versus a GPU, which can hash 120 megahashes per second. (One terahash per second (TH/s) is equal to 1 trillion hashes; 1 megahash per second (MH/s) is equal to 1 million hashes.) A hash is a hexadecimal number generated by the interaction between the microprocessor and its accompanying algorithm. As a result, ASICs have taken over the Bitcoin mining realm.

When it comes to mining, the processor's ability to solve the puzzles is paramount. As a general rule, the hardier the processor, the more likely your chances of success.

ASICs is the latest and the greatest technology for crypto mining. But it comes with significant advantages and disadvantages. As an individual miner, your biggest decisions involve the costs and the logistics of setting up a rig weighted against the potential profit. This entry offers details to help you sort through the process.

INSIDE THE HASHING PROCESS

An ASICs processor is placed on an integrated circuit board and programmed to generate hashes based on the instructions of its algorithm. The goal is to generate two specific numbers (the nonce and the extra nonce), which are the solutions to the puzzle. This is a highly intensive computing process that generates a great amount of heat, which requires aggressive forms of cooling, essentially making ASICs mining at home prohibitively expensive and highly impractical.

Here are some factors to review when considering whether ASICs mining will work for you:

- ASICs miners are loud and generate a great amount of heat, so be careful with choosing a home setup.
- ASICs rigs consume a lot of power, which can impact your electricity bill.
- ASICs miners have a limited number of coins that they can mine. These include bitcoin (BTC), Litecoin (LTC), Dogecoin (DOGE), Dash (DASH), Zcash (ZEC), and Ethereum Classic (ETC).
  - Bitcoin and Litecoin are considered very difficult to mine. Dogecoin, Ethereum Classic, Zcash, and Dash are considered easy to moderately difficult. Dogecoin has the highest reward potential, but its low value per coin counters this.
  - Compare the up-front and maintenance costs (including electricity and possible space rental) to the potential rewards; consider whether the first outweighs the second. You can always join a pool to increase your reward potential and reduce your costs.

THE BEST ASICS MINERS

Hash rates are measured in hashes per second (H/s). It follows the metric system and is the most reliable method of measuring the ability of an ASIC miner to deliver the goods. The most powerful ASICs for Bitcoin are measured in terahash, where 1 terahash equals 1 trillion hashes (1 TH=1,000,000,000,000 hashes). To choose the best ASIC miner, pick the one with the lowest hash speed, as it will use less electricity and be more cost-effective. Also consider its noise production. Here is an illustrative sampling of the leading ASICs miners available as of August 2025, including their costs and power consumption:

- The Bitmain Antminer S21e XP Hyd 3U generates 860 TH/s, consuming 11,180 watts, and may cost as much as $4,000 to purchase, although prices can vary due to supply and demand, as well as the emergence of new versions. This applies to all miners.
- The Bitmain Antminer S21 XP+ Hyd generates 500 TH/s, consuming 5,500 watts, and costs $12,700.
- The Auradine Teraflux AH3880 generates 600 TH/s, consuming 8,700 watts, and costs $7,800.
- Bitdeer SealMiner A2 Pro Hyd generates 500 TH/s, consuming 7,450 watts, and costs $3,958.
- The MicroBT WhatsMiner M66S++ generates 356 TH/s, consuming 5,518 watts, and costs $8,660.

The Bitmain miners are the most efficient but are also the most expensive. The other three options are almost identical in their efficiency ratings, which means the Bitdeer is likely the best deal from a purely financial and efficiency standpoint.

In addition, the Bitmain Antminer S21e XP Hyd 3U is considered to be the quietest and lowest heat-producing unit in the group. The Bitmain Antminer S21 XP+ Hyd is best suited for very competitive mining environments (like Bitcoin). The Auradine model may be suited for a home setup. On the other hand, the MicroBT model is noisy and may be best suited for a data center–type setup.

ASICs Slow Growth

ASICs technology development has slowed. Rather than introducing new versions of the technology, manufacturers are currently focused on practical aspects such as reducing the size, heat, and noise production of the units. Hydrocooling is an excellent noise reduction method. In the end, you must decide between up-front, maintenance, and set-up costs and the potential for profitability.

SOLO MINING

Sailing on Your Own

Deciding if you're going to mine crypto solo or via a pool is an important question to answer. If you decide to be a solo miner, you're willing to assume all the risks and potential rewards of mining crypto by yourself. That means that you'll have to make all the important decisions, shoulder all the costs, and reap all the potential rewards, potential setbacks, and the reality that you may fail all by yourself.

At its core, solo mining means that you will validate transactions, update blockchains, and receive all potential benefits via your own rig. You'll be responsible for doing all the research on equipment and related infrastructure, the location for your mining business, and conducting the cost, benefit, and likelihood of profitability. You may employ consultants, scour the Internet for information, and ask other miners about their experience, but, in the end, the final decision and the potential outcomes will be on you.

SURVIVING SOLO MINING

The major advantages for solo mining are the independence it provides and the potential for rewards. These are countered by the increased competition in mining and the potentially prohibitive costs involved for the average person. That said, here are some excellent ways to increase your chances of being successful with a solo mining operation:

1. First, make sure to choose the right hardware. It might cost you a bit up front, but getting the right miner hardware is a huge step in the right direction. You can start off slow with a GPU setup, but if you're serious, it makes sense to consider an ASICs rig. There are some cheaper models out there (like Bitmain Antminer) that you can get for around $1,600, or less if you get a refurbished model.

2. Then, move to downloading and configuring the right software that is compatible with your system and the coins you're planning to mine. Two user-friendly programs to consider are CGMiner or BFGMiner. The installation is often completed within minutes.

3. Set up your wallet and connect your hardware to the Bitcoin network or your selected mining pool. To join the Bitcoin network, you download a Bitcoin client (a software program that allows your rig to interact with the Bitcoin or another selected network) onto your rig.

4. Consider setting up a real-time monitoring program. This allows you to monitor your rig's actions and lets you fine-tune its operation. For example, you can track your hash rates, your rig's temperature, and automate rig functions to optimize performance. Make sure that the software works with your setup's hardware before the download.

5. Optimize your network with the best possible router and Internet connection. Be obsessive about all your cables and your power supply being tightly connected.

6. Get the best network security program you can afford. Set it up ahead of your foray into mining and update regularly.

7. Keep a close eye on costs, especially power and maintenance costs. Something as small as a dusty fan could hamper your chances of scoring rewards.

8. Always be on the lookout for any technology that will make your rig faster, more efficient, and cost-effective. One option is to use artificial intelligence (AI) to help your rig sort through the possibilities of the blockchain. Two uses that can add up quickly are using AI to optimize your algorithms via monitoring blockchain conditions and liquidity (the amount of money circulating in the system at any one time). The higher the liquidity, the better the potential of being successful. Another is to use it to optimize power consumption.

9. Most of all, be realistic about your returns. You're up against big competition with hundreds of very advanced rigs in well-electrified, climate-controlled data centers. When you hit success points, try to figure out how you did it and try to replicate the technique.

When to Join a Pool

Give yourself time to see if you can be successful. If you're struggling and your returns are less than what you were expecting, it's a good time to explore a mining pool. Even though your rewards may be smaller, your odds of success are likely to be higher and more consistent.

POOL MINING

Taming the Race

The competition to mine coins is a race that, in many cases, is tilted to the players that have the most computing power and the capital to stay in the game and capture the rewards. This competitive landscape led to the formation of mining pools.

A mining pool is a group of crypto miners who pool their computational resources and share the rewards when the pool successfully mines a block of cryptocurrency. The rewards are split based on the contribution of each individual participant to the pool's success in mining each individual block. Mining pools are formed via the connection of individuals, via a network, to the pool.

SETTING UP AND GETTING STARTED

Once you've set up your mining rig hardware, software, and wallet, you can join a mining pool. There are plenty of them out there and each one has different characteristics. It makes sense to research as many as possible before making the leap into your first one. And just because you choose one, there's no rule that says you have to stick with it or use it exclusively. If it doesn't work for you, it's a good idea to move to one that suits your goals better.

Aside from important factors like security and user-friendliness, it's important to know how you're going to get paid, specifically how much and how often. Getting paid involves either fees or rewards (new coins) for each block you've successfully mined. Once you've decided, you register on the platform, create an account, and link your mining rig to the platform following the instructions, which may vary. Payments are delivered to your account based on the platform's schedule, which may be anywhere from daily to periodically depending on the platform's rules. Always check for your rig's software compatibility, and be aware of the payment schedule before you create your account and try to link your rig to it.

Once everything is set up and functional, you can start the mining process. The platform's dashboard will let you monitor the activity of your account and keep up with your progress and earnings.

GETTING REWARDS

Reward payoffs are distributed either via a Pay-Per-Share (PPS) or Pay-Per-Last-N-Shares (PPLNS) system. Under PPS, miners receive rewards based on their contribution (the number of shares they own in the pool) to solving the crypto puzzle. PPLNS rewards are distributed based on the last shares submitted (the computing power a miner contributes to solving the block) before the block puzzle was solved. More specifically, PPLNS rewards are based on the number of shares submitted by each miner during each individual round of mining. In other words, if you contributed 10% of the computing power that solved the puzzle, you receive 10% of the rewards.

PPLNS is an attempt to prevent or reduce pool hopping (promoting loyalty among the members of the pool). On the other hand, the rewards may be unpredictable. In contrast, PPS rewards are based on the number of shares submitted by any miner, whether a block is found or not. So, you know what you're going to be paid ahead of time. PPS encourages miners to switch pools when the individual pool that they've chosen has a low success rate. The pool operator is at a higher risk of capital loss in PPS, as it pays for participation versus success. The flip side is that PPS pools tend to charge miners higher fees to compensate for the potential capital loss inherent to the model. PPLNS does offer the potential for more stable income, as there is often a loyalty incentive.

Regardless of the reward structure, each pool has its own policies and methods of paying out rewards. For example, a popular PPS pool known as F2Pool (F2Pool.zendesk.com) pays rewards daily from 0:00 to 8:00 UTC (Universal Time). This type of system benefits miners who value predictability and count on the income for expenses.

Platform Details

A well-known PPLNS platform, WoolyPooly (https://woolypooly.com) pays out as soon as the minimum payout amount is reached for individual miners. You set up the minimum threshold payout you'd like when you register to use the pool (registration is optional), and you can adjust it accordingly. WoolyPooly offers tools to help you track your payout progress.

When it comes to PPLNS platforms, WoolyPooly specializes in altcoins, as does 2Miners (https://2miners.com). Braiins Pool (https://braiins.com/pool), Nanopool (https://nanopool.org), and MiningPoolHub (https://miningpoolhub.com) offer access to mining of various cryptocurrencies.

For PPS platforms, F2Pool, Antpool (www.antpool.com), and BTC.com (https://btc.com) offer access to various cryptocurrency mining opportunities. Cruxpool (https://cruxpool.com) offers access to altcoin mining.

Succeed with Pool Mining

The key to success with pool crypto mining is to set some goals, monitor your progress, and remain flexible. If your goal is to produce $300 in rewards per month and you're falling short of it consistently, review your process. Start by considering the amount of computing power you're contributing to the platform; whether you're mining the best coin for your system and the blockchain you're trying to access; and whether the reward distribution system works for you. Depending on your findings, you can act accordingly by switching platforms or adjusting your methods at each step of the way.

Chapter 6

Investing In Cryptocurrency

When compared to investing in other asset classes like stocks, investing in crypto has both inherent similarities and unique differences. The similarities are intuitive; you put your money in, and it grows or it falls in value depending on the market.

The differences, however, are stark. When it comes to crypto, there's a lot to take in. Aside from the basic concepts—like crypto being a way to preserve the value of your assets against inflation and to make transactions—this currency is a purely technological and highly complex space, rife with its own rules and intricacies. Plus, there's an ever-growing number of exchanges, platforms, coins, and tokens. Additionally, while this is changing daily, large portions of the crypto universe remain unregulated, raising the risk of fraud and misunderstanding. As a result, this chapter offers a tangible and executable approach to investing in crypto by applying what's adaptable from other asset classes and combining it with tactics exclusive to this new investment realm.

FOUNDATIONS OF INVESTING

Important Steps Before You Start

If you're like most people interested in investing, you're excited and ready to go. You can't wait to set up your crypto wallet and get started. But before starting your investment endeavor in crypto, or in any other asset class, it's a good idea to have your financial house in order. You'll need to think about what you're trying to accomplish by investing in crypto and how you're going to use the proceeds. Once you've figured these two important points out, you can proceed to crafting a trading plan.

Here are the most important basic steps and required knowledge to become a crypto investor. These principles are, in many ways, applicable to investing in any asset class, whether it's the stock market, crypto, or real estate.

YOUR PERSONAL BALANCE SHEET

The goal with this step is to ensure you have enough money so that you can take the risks involved in becoming a crypto investor. First, look at your monthly budget and see how much you have left over when all your bills are paid (cash flow positive status). If you have money left over, you've cleared the first hurdle. If you don't have any spare funds, don't be discouraged. Review the areas that you can adjust and give yourself some time to get the necessary changes accomplished. Meanwhile, see where you can squeeze out a few bucks here and there and start putting together a potential crypto stash that you can deploy at some point.

Crypto should not be your primary source of income unless your plan is to become a full-time crypto trader. So, if you're like most people, crypto is going to be a method of diversifying your investment portfolio. Thus, before risking your money, pay special attention to fully funding your retirement fund and make sure other important financial provisions for your family and for your future are covered. Review all your expenses, including student loans and future college expenses for yourself or family members. Don't forget about vacations and other things that matter.

Side Hustles Can Push You Financially Forward

If you're particularly entrepreneurial, you may want to consider developing a side hustle in order to raise funds to put in your crypto wallet. You can try the common ones such as DoorDash, Uber, and Lyft, or use your talents such as offering your services as a coach or tutor in an area where you're an expert.

UNDERSTAND YOUR MARKET

Once you review your balance sheet, you should understand the basics of all markets and how the crypto market compares. Whereas stocks, bonds, and commodities have their own sets of rules as well as internal and external factors that affect prices, crypto prices are affected by only two influences: supply and demand of any coin, and the liquidity in the system. Both of those factors are intertwined by the general mood of the investors and the general price trend that is unfolding at any time.

Under normal circumstances, interest rates, corporate earnings, and the supply and demand of commodities have a very low influence on the price of cryptocurrencies. Crypto prices fluctuate based mostly on what the demand for coins is at any moment (whether due to transaction, investing, or speculation) and how much money is available in the financial system to allocate to crypto trading.

SET INVESTMENT GOALS

The best trading plans are actionable and easy to implement. Start with a goal: This shouldn't be a financial goal, like being a millionaire in five years. Instead, start with a defined goal based on how you're going to use your crypto profits. Examples of defined goals include producing current income, building long-term wealth, or a combination of both.

Generating Income Through Investing

If you're focusing on producing current income, you might be better served by short-term trading tactics that produce smaller profits in hours or days. This approach requires the knowledge to do technical analyses of price charts and a significant time commitment to find the proper setups on these charts, which are likely to lead to profitable trades.

Generally speaking, this type of approach is best guided by setting a goal, such as closing out positions when they've delivered $100 in gains. You might then add a goal of repeating similar trades four or five times per month in order to produce, for example, $500 of gains to save or spend on a recurring expense (a car payment, for example).

LONG-TERM WEALTH BUILDING PLAN

If your goal is to build long-term wealth through crypto, then you have to develop some patience and craft a plan that incorporates both a savings component and an asset allocation component. You can do this in multiple ways, which will be discussed in detail later in this chapter. The key to success with this approach is to be consistent and to keep a long-term focus while avoiding being overwhelmed by the daily price fluctuations of bitcoin, ether, and the rest of the coins.

Of course, you can opt to use stablecoins as a savings vehicle, and to rely on lending your coins as a way to earn interest and grow your savings. Whichever method you choose, don't make crypto the sole asset in your portfolio, and stay consistent and remain patient.

UNDERSTAND AND ACCEPT RISK

Finally, as an investor, you appreciate the fact that there is risk involved. You know that regardless of how good you are with understanding crypto, there will be periods where you most likely will lose money; you have no control over the market. The best anyone can hope for, even large investors, is that they can catch the waves of rising prices long enough to come out of the period with more money than what they put in.

TECHNICAL ANALYSIS

Don't Trade Without Price Charts

Trading crypto, or any other market, without understanding the basics of price chart analysis (technical analysis) is a sure way to lose money. This entry covers the minimum requirements of technical analysis of price charts.

WHERE TO FIND PRICE CHARTS

When looking to do some price chart analysis, the first step is to find a reliable price chart service that offers crypto price charts. One of them is StockCharts.com, which offers a full charting service. You can select multiple time frames such as intraday, daily, or weekly charts. If you have a brokerage account, such as with Robinhood or Fidelity, you can access price charts through their platform. You can also access free cryptocurrency charts online through sites such as CoinMarketCap (https://coinmarketcap.com), or Investing .com (www.investing.com). Crypto exchanges, such as Coinbase, offer price charts along with tutorials (www.coinbase.com/learn/advanced-trading/reading-financial-charts).

TYPES OF PRICE CHARTS

There are three basic types of price charts: candlestick charts, bar charts, and line charts. Line charts are the least commonly used for trading, but they can be useful to examine long-term trends. Each one has its pros and cons, as explained here.

Candlestick Charts

Candlestick charts have two parts, the thick candle (body) and the wick (thin lines above or below the body). The thick portion depicts where the price opened and closed on the day. The thin portion(s) shows you the high and low price of the day. There are many important patterns candlestick charts depict that can predict future price trends, and pro traders tend to favor these charts.

Bar Charts

Bar charts are also known as open-high-low-close (OHLC) charts and are similar in content to candlestick charts. The major difference is that candlesticks have a more robust appearance due to the thick body portion, while bar charts are thinner in appearance. Both charts are useful, and you should try them both before developing a preference.

Line Charts

Line charts are of limited use in trading because they *only* display the closing price. Your analysis is incomplete without knowing the trading range for the day. For this reason, they may be a less desirable option, and it's recommended to use one of the other types instead.

IMPORTANT PRICE CHART INDICATORS

To trade, you must familiarize yourself with four basic categories of indicators with multiple individual participants in several categories. Each one of them offers you a glimpse into the status of both the current price and the trend.

Overbought/Oversold Indicators

This group of indicators tells you when an asset, including crypto, has been sold (oversold) or bought (overbought) so aggressively that a change in the trend is likely. The indicator won't tell you when the trend change will happen, but it will alert you that the odds of it occurring are increasing. Popular oversold/overbought indicators include the relative strength index (RSI) and the moving average convergence/divergence (MACD) indicator.

Support and Resistance Indicators

Support refers to a price area where an asset holds after a price drop. Support areas often lead to the formation of a price base (a sideways consolidation of the price). Price consolidations are often the prelude to a rebound in prices. Price support is often confirmed by oversold readings in indicators such as RSI and MACD.

Resistance is the opposite of support and signifies a price area that prices are struggling to rise above. When prices fail to rise above resistance, they either consolidate before resuming their climb, or reverse and fall. Resistance areas are often confirmed by overbought readings in indicators such as RSI and MACD.

Volume-by-Price Bars

Volume-by-price (VBP) bars are depicted as large horizontal bars (histograms) plotted along the y-axis in price charts. They are a useful visual cue that highlights important areas where trading is very active. As with any histogram, the larger the bar, the more indicative of its importance as a support or resistance level. The presence of large VBP bars (which extend into the price chart for a long distance) or clusters of multiple bars are particularly important, as they indicate that trading activity is very aggressive at these price levels. When prices rise above or fall below large bar clusters, they usually indicate that the emerging trend is very meaningful.

Moving Averages

Perhaps the most popular indicators on price charts are moving averages. These indicators are visualized by lines constructed by the average price of an asset over a period of time (minutes, days, or weeks). The average price for the period is plotted, and a line results when the subsequent dots are plotted in sequence. Popular moving averages are the ten-, twenty-, fifty-, and two-hundred-day moving averages. When prices rise above or fall below a moving average, they signal a potential change in the price trend.

Volatility Bands

Volatility bands (or Bollinger Bands) were created by John Bollinger and are available on most charting services. They are visible above and below the price trend, and they are built on a formula based on a moving average. The most common construct is that of the twenty-day moving average and volatility bands based on two standard deviations above and below the moving average (the basis for the calculation of the standard deviations). Together, this combination of indicators depicts price action two standard deviations above and two standard deviations below the moving average.

When prices rise above the upper band or fall below the lower band, they signal a potential reversal in the trend. When the bands close in on the moving average (or the "band squeeze"), it's a sign that a big move in the price is likely, though the direction is unknown.

Money Flow Indicators

Money flow indicators tell you when money is flowing into or out of assets. They are useful confirmers of price trends. Ideally you want to see prices rising along with rising money flow indicators. If prices are rising and money flow indicators are falling, it's considered to be a warning sign for a potential price top, a price point near which a negative price drop or reversal is likely to happen. If money flow indicators are rising and prices are falling or moving sideways, it's a sign that money is quietly moving into an asset. Three useful money flow indicators are the accumulation/distribution indicator (ADI), the on-balance volume (OBV) line, and the aptly named Money Flow Index (MFI). Reputable charting services provide all three.

What Is Included on a Thorough Price Chart?

A proper price chart includes support and resistance, moving averages, Bollinger Bands, money flow, and overbought and oversold indicators. When you put them all together, you're able to discern whether money is moving into or out of the underlying asset pictured on the price chart. From a trading standpoint, the odds of success rise when you follow the direction of the money flow.

HOW TO TRADE BITCOIN USING TECHNICAL ANALYSIS

A Detailed Method for Trading Bitcoin from the Ground Up

The best way to illustrate any concept is to provide a concise and granular example. This section describes a hypothetical Bitcoin trade based on real-time pricing data from the summer of 2025. The primary goal is to illustrate the thought process and an actionable execution method. The trade assumes that you have $150,000 cash in your crypto wallet for trading; this is purely for illustrative purposes. You can adjust your trades based on your own resources. What's important are the concepts through which you approach the trade. This sample trade will be based on a $100,000 asset transfer.

This trade is designed as part of a long-term, wealth-building strategy, which implies that you will cash in your profits and return them to a cash equivalent account, where you can wait for the next trading opportunity.

A PURELY TECHNICAL BITCOIN TRADE

In a trade, your first step is to look at the general price trend. Are prices rising, falling, or moving sideways? Start by looking at a daily price chart covering a full year of trading activity. For example, during the period of late July 2024 to late July 2025, Bitcoin rose from $50,000 to $118,000. There were two major rallies, one frightening decline (the price dropped from $110,000 to $75,000 in four months), and three periods of consolidation. The consolidation periods roughly ranged from three to four months while the rallies lasted roughly four to six weeks before pausing. Each transition from one phase to another followed precise technical presentations based on the following indicators (note: You can learn more about these indicators in the previous entry, "Technical Analysis"):

- **Overbought/oversold indicators:** The price tops, which preceded negative price reversals, followed overbought readings (above 70) on the RSI indicator, while the bottoms (price points that preceded positive price reversals) followed oversold readings on RSI (readings of 30 or below). RSI is useful as both a momentum and a price reversal indicator. Its general trend (up or down) indicates the general price trend. A reading of 30, or below, indicates that the market is oversold and will eventually bounce and move higher. A move above or below 50 confirms the direction of prices. A reading of 70 or above suggests the market is overbought and ripe for a downward price reversal. Each bottom required two tests of the low prices for the decline, with the second bottom registering a higher RSI reading than the first low. This signals that the second bottom has less downside momentum than the first bottom and is the spot where you start buying.

- **Support and resistance indicators:** Each bottom occurred at the bottom range of a cluster (shelf) of VBP bars, while the top before the scary decline occurred near the top of a large VBP bar cluster. Thus, paying attention to support and resistance is crucial, as support that holds offers a plausible entry point for a trade, while resistance that fails offers a potential exit point for a trade.

- **Moving averages:** Rallies accelerated when the price moved above the twenty- and fifty-day moving averages. Selling ensued when the price broke below the twenty- and fifty-day moving averages. Long lasting rallies followed breaks above the two-hundred-day moving average. The scary decline found support just below its two-hundred-day moving average.
- **Volatility bands:** Each major move, up or down, was preceded by a "squeeze" of the volatility bands. Reversals began after the price breached the upper or lower band.
- **Money flow indicators:** Both the ADI and OBV lines rose short term during rallies and pulled back during declines as money moved in and out of Bitcoin. On a longer-term viewing, the ADI rose steadily throughout the whole year while the OBV line rose with rallies and rolled over during declines.

Technical analysis simplifies trading decisions by offering a visual status of the current price action. Becoming proficient in the use of this skill set will pay off in the short and in the long run.

Putting It All Together

Once the technical parts line up, your next step is to decide how you will enter the trade. You can buy in all at once based on your preferred method, such as when the price crosses above a specific moving average, when the prices rise above a crucial VBP bar highlighted resistance level, or a combination of conditions. You should practice through paper trading (trading without spending real money and monitoring how certain conditions could affect your investments).

Consider a gradual entry. You buy one third of your position when Bitcoin rises above the twenty-day moving average, another third when it crosses the fifty-day, and the final third when it crosses above the two-hundred-day. Use VBP bars as guides and figure out which approach suits you best.

You had two opportunities to trade Bitcoin for a period of four to eight weeks depending on your approach. Each opportunity delivered profits, with the first entry in November 2024 at $60,000 delivering a $30,000 profit upon exit in February 2025 at $90,000. The second trade had you re-enter at $90,000 still open as of late July, with the price starting to consolidate around $120,000, offering an opportunity to take profits by reducing the size of the position.

HODLing for Profits

If you chose to HODL during this period, you were also well rewarded. You made money on paper, even during the volatile April period where the price dropped from $105,000 to $75,000 before rebounding.

Think of the two-hundred-day moving average as the dividing line between long-term uptrends and down trends. In this context, technical analysis—especially keeping track of prices in relation to the two-hundred-day moving average—would have been useful as the October 2024–March 2025 rally started when Bitcoin rose above its two-hundred-day moving average. Plus, the pullback in prices that extended from late 2024 until the spring of 2025 found support near the two-hundred-day moving average. Had you bought at the bottom, near $60,000, and held on throughout the entire period, you would still be sitting on a $60,000 gain, having doubled your money by HODLing.

The Advantage of Visual Analysis

Trading or HODLing go better with price charts. The take-home message is that because Bitcoin (and all crypto coins) trade purely on the supply and demand and liquidity status of the market, the visual analysis and entry and exit cues are critical to your decision-making process, regardless of whether you have a short, intermediate, or long-term time frame.

CRYPTO OPTIONS

An Evolving and Risky Way to Trade

The options market in stocks dwarfs the stock market in both volume and the amount of money that trades in it. Because of its popularity in other markets, it has expanded its appeal to crypto. That said, crypto options (options contracts with cryptocurrencies as the underlying assets), like all options, offer both high levels of rewards and even higher levels of risk to contend with.

This entry offers a glimpse into crypto options, but it is *not* comprehensive. The goal here is to provide essential tools to illustrate the intricacies of crypto options. Trading crypto is challenging without the added knowledge required to trade options. So, do more extensive research on options trading before you take the plunge.

OPTIONS BASICS

Options are derivatives (financial contracts) that are based on an underlying asset. A call option contract gives the buyer the right to buy a predetermined quantity of the underlying asset at a set price (the strike price) by a specific date (the expiration date). A put option gives the holder an obligation to sell a predetermined quantity of the underlying asset at the strike price by the expiration date For example, a bitcoin option's underlying asset is one bitcoin, thus giving traders access to the standard call and put option rights and obligations applicable to Bitcoin through options.

Options are priced at a fraction of the underlying asset and are leveraged, meaning that the percentage gains or losses of options are multiples of those of the underlying asset. Given that crypto is inherently volatile, crypto options multiply the volatility of the underlying coin.

While you can trade stock options through your discount broker, to trade crypto options, you need an options trading account at a crypto exchange, where you can use options as a trading vehicle. Three trusted crypto options trading platforms are Binance, Bybit, and Crypto.com. Each exchange has its own set of requirements and rules regarding crypto options trading. You may also have to meet local, regional, and country specific requirements.

The allure of crypto options is that the inherent volatility of the underlying coins is further amplified by the potential volatility of options as a trading instrument. Of course, volatility is a double-edged sword, meaning that you can make extraordinary gains via crypto options, but the trades that go against you could deliver big losses.

CALLS AND PUTS

There are two types of options, call options and put options. Call options bet on higher prices as they appreciate in value when the underlying asset rises and lose value when the underlying asset falls in price. Put options bet on falling prices; they rise in value when the underlying asset falls in price and lose value when the underlying asset's price rises.

HELPFUL TERMINOLOGY

To trade options, you must become familiar with these important terms:

- **Option premium** describes the cost of the option. When you buy options (speculative trade) you pay a premium. When you sell an option, you collect a premium (income-producing trade).
- **Strike price** is the price above for calls, below for puts where an option becomes "in the money" (ITM). In the money options trade on a dollar per dollar basis with the underlying asset. Thus, a one-dollar gain in Bitcoin would trigger a one-dollar gain in a Bitcoin call option that is above its strike price and a Bitcoin put option would do the opposite. For example, a December 2025 $100,000 bitcoin call option would be in the money if BTC was trading at $101,000. At a bitcoin price of $100,000 it would be "at the money" (ATM) and at $999,999 it would be "out of the money" (OTM). If your option is ITM, you have the right to buy (exercise) bitcoin at $100,000 (the strike price) and sell it at the market price any time up to the expiration date. You can also sell the option for the current market price, which will also likely deliver a profit if the option is in the money. You can close out your option position at any time whether it's in the money or not. When you close an option position you may incur gains or losses depending on the price progression after you opened the option position.
- **Expiration date** is the date at which an option stops trading. If the option is ITM (meaning it's above its strike price) on the expiration date, it may be exercised or assigned. If the option is

OTM, it expires worthless. If the option is ATM on the expiration date, it will likely expire worthless.

- **Time value** is the portion of the price of the option that is based on how much time there is to expiration. An option with three months to expiration has a higher time value than one with one month to expiration.

While it can take some time to master options, a great place to start is by getting comfortable with the applicable terminology of this useful asset class.

BUYING AND SELLING OPTIONS

Buying options is relatively straightforward. For example, if you're expecting the price of Ethereum to rise, you may buy a call option. When you buy an Ethereum put option, you're expecting the price to fall.

Selling options can be done with or without owning the underlying asset. You can sell calls, or you can sell puts and collect premium. Selling covered calls (collecting premium when you own the underlying crypto) is a useful strategy during a flat or falling market but should be avoided when prices are rising. Selling puts (with or without owning the underlying coin) is best during flat or rising markets.

The inherent risk of selling options is that you may face assignment. Remember an options contract gives the buyer a set of rights and the seller a set of obligations. Assignment is when the buyer exercises their rights by triggering your obligation. When you sell a call and it rises above the strike price, the buyer may exercise their right to buy the crypto at the strike price. You keep the premium but have to sell the crypto at the strike price. When you sell a put option and it falls below the strike price, the buyer may exercise their right and buy the crypto at the strike price. You keep the premium but take a loss on the difference between the strike price and the price of the put at exercise.

Before You Trade Options

Crypto options offer the opportunity to speculate or receive income via targeted options strategies. Options trading is best conducted by experienced traders. If you decide to try your luck, you must become well versed in risk management, diligently paper trade, and review past trade results before committing real money.

CRYPTO FUTURES

The First Validators of Crypto

You might be surprised to know that the first validation of crypto, outside of its cult following as an asset class, came from the futures market. In 2017, both the Chicago Mercantile Exchange (CME) and the Chicago Board Options Exchange (CBOE) launched futures contracts based on crypto. The event gave the crypto universe a boost, thrusting it into the mainstream financial markets and legitimized it as a viable asset class. This entry gives a look at how crypto futures work, the different types, and more.

FUTURES BASICS

A crypto futures contract is an agreement between a buyer and seller for a predetermined price at a standardized date. All participants in a particular crypto futures contract are held to the same settlement date. Crypto futures contracts are settled in cash or by delivery of the crypto-currency to your wallet at the closing price on the expiration date.

You can use crypto futures to hedge positions (provide some safety against loss) or as a speculative bet on the direction of the underlying crypto. You can buy crypto futures contracts if the price of coins is expected to rise, or you can sell futures contracts short in expectations of the price of the underlying crypto falling. A short sale is when you borrow a contract from the broker in hopes that it will fall in price. If it does, you can buy it back at the lower price and keep the difference between the original sale price and the price at which you purchased the contract as your profit. Short selling is very risky under normal circumstances when applied to non-crypto assets like stocks. It's even riskier in crypto and is not advisable for beginners.

Crypto futures contracts are highly leveraged, are often more volatile in their price fluctuations than the underlying cryptocurrency, and require a margin account. A margin account requires that a certain amount of money is available to cover the value of the contracts held. When the amount falls below the margin requirement, you are required to put up more money to cover the deficit. If you aren't able to do so, the exchange will close your position to cover the debt.

Crypto futures trading requires that you set up an account through which you make the transactions. The details are beyond the scope of this book, but you should not execute any futures trades without being fully versed in the process, as there are important capital requirements and a specific set of protocols to execute the trades. You can get precise details at https://socialcapitalmarkets.net/crypto-trading/futures.

Types of Futures Contracts

There are two types of crypto futures contracts: standard and perpetual. Standard contracts have expiration dates. Perpetual contracts do not and can be held for extended periods of time.

Perpetual contracts include a funding rate, which is a periodic payment system to keep the contract open. Funding rates vary based on the current status of the market. When the futures price is above the spot price (the current market price) of the currency, buyers pay sellers. When the price falls below the spot price, sellers pay the buyers.

The funding rate is calculated based on interest rates set by the exchange and the premium index, which is the difference between the futures price and the spot price of the underlying crypto. The funding rate is adjusted periodically.

WHERE TO TRADE CRYPTO FUTURES

You can trade crypto futures at multiple locations. Trading them at the CME makes sense, since that's the place where these trades started, and they are a regulated, highly reputable futures exchange with high liquidity and stability. Binance and BitMEX are also considered fine places to trade crypto futures.

TYPES OF CRYPTO FUTURES

Aside from the types of futures contracts, there are also many types of crypto futures. Each has its own pros and cons, and you should do more research before committing. Here are some common crypto futures available to trade:

- Bitcoin futures are popular due to the market dominance and liquidity of the underlying coin.
- Ethereum futures are also popular and liquid.
- Litecoin futures are preferred by some traders due to a rapid execution rate.

There are other futures contracts based on crypto that are available to trade. These include Polkadot, LINK, and Uniswap futures. Yet, given the inherent risk of cryptocurrencies, which is magnified further via the construct of futures contracts, beginners should hold off on trading in this area until they gain experience. And as with any new trading endeavor, the first steps should be in highly liquid markets after carefully studying the subject matter and putting in the time to paper trade (a practice form of trading without investing any real money).

Futures As a Speculative Trade

If you're expecting a rise in bitcoin but don't have the $100,000+ to buy a coin (and you don't want to bother with satoshis), you can buy a Bitcoin futures contract. If you buy at the right time and the price rises, you can sell the contract before expiration and pocket the profit. If you hold the contract to expiration, you will then receive delivery of the bitcoin specified in the contract after expiration. In this way, you may buy bitcoin at a discount.

Futures As a Hedge

Let's say you have a spot position in Bitcoin (a position which you can buy or sell at current prices) and you notice the price is starting to weaken. As a hedge (a way to protect your current crypto assets against losses) you may consider selling a futures contract short. If you're right and the price of your crypto holdings fall, the price of your futures contract should also fall. Because you sold the contract, you can buy it back at a lower price and your profit is the difference between your entry price and your selling price. This helps reduce any loss in your actual crypto holdings.

STEPS REQUIRED TO TRADE CRYPTO FUTURES

Given the previous information, you should have a basic understanding on what futures are and what types may work for you. The next step is actually following the process required to trade crypto futures:

1. **Research and select a reputable platform.** Start by reviewing CME and compare it to others you may consider; Bybit, BingX, and Binance are usually near the top of futures trading platform rankings.
2. **Create an account.** Follow the steps to create an account with your chosen platform. Remember that identity verification is required.
3. **Fund the account.** The margin may require further funding if the market goes against you.
4. **Familiarize yourself with the order platform.** You should know how to protect yourself by using the right types of orders applicable to your goals.
5. **Learn about stop-loss orders and other protective orders and how they impact your trading.** A stop-loss order is an instruction to automatically sell a security if the price falls to a specific price; this can help mitigate losses. You can get the full details on protecting your trades via protective measures such as stop-losses at www.investopedia.com/terms/s/stoporder.asp.

Why So Risky?

Crypto futures are high-risk investments by construct because they leverage the already leveraged and volatile cryptocurrencies. It is also the premise used to speculate and hedge by hedge funds and large institutions, which further increases the risk, especially for beginner investors.

CRYPTO ETFS

A Simpler Way to Trade Crypto

An exchange-traded fund (ETF) is a great way to trade crypto without having to open a specialized account at a crypto exchange or to expand the trading abilities of your brokerage account at Robinhood or Fidelity. That's because you can trade ETFs just as you trade stocks.

But just because they are convenient, it doesn't mean that you shouldn't pay attention to the underlying crypto or the market conditions. On the other hand, if you have a good handle of the price trend for bitcoin or ether, a crypto ETF is a great way to participate in the crypto markets. Plus, you can trade both crypto futures and spot cryptocurrencies via ETFs, and crypto ETFs also offer options. By using the ETF instead of directly investing in crypto, you may be able to simplify the jurisdictional and tax consequences directly related to crypto.

Perhaps the best characteristic of ETFs is that they are designed to follow the trend of the asset in which they invest. So, well-structured Bitcoin ETFs rise and fall based on the price of bitcoin, which means that if you apply the price chart analysis and trading methods described in the technical analysis sections mentioned in this chapter to ETFs, you're all set.

PROMINENT BITCOIN ETFS

The first crypto ETFs were approved by the SEC in 2024 and featured both Bitcoin and Ethereum. These funds are great when you get started, as many of them follow the trend in their underlying currency faithfully. By the same token, it's important to research the fund's holdings, its relationships, and their ability to follow the trend of the underlying cryptocurrency. Some "crypto" ETFs don't invest in crypto directly.

The iShares Bitcoin Trust ETF (IBIT) went public in January 2024 and is often the most liquid and active Bitcoin ETF. It uses Coinbase technology to manage its price action. It's designed to rise and fall with the price of bitcoin and easily meets the goal. This is a great way to indirectly participate in the price of bitcoin. IBIT also offers highly liquid options that can be traded for speculation, hedging, or income production.

The Grayscale Bitcoin Trust (GBTC), debuting in 2025, was an early entrant into the crypto ETF world. Its value rises and falls based on the rise and fall of the number of bitcoin coins it owns minus expenses. It follows the general price trend of its underlying assets (bitcoin) and has a long-term record that is easily reviewed. Its initial value was near $0.30, and in late July 2025, it traded above $100. You can also trade GBTC options.

The ProShares Bitcoin ETF (BITO) was established in 2021, and it trades Bitcoin futures. Because it doesn't invest directly in bitcoin, it can be a bit quirky in the short term. Over time, however, its price trend closely follows that of bitcoin. It also offers options trading.

The Valkyrie Bitcoin Miners ETF (WGMI) invests in companies that mine bitcoin. It tends to follow the general trend of bitcoin's price but is also subject to the performance of its holdings in bitcoin miners. These companies, in many cases, are small international companies and their earnings are not as predictable as large cap technology stocks such as Amazon.com. Thus, the volatility in this ETF's daily prices, especially in earnings season, can be more than what you see in pure Bitcoin-investing ETFs. WGMI offers options.

The Schwab Crypto Thematic ETF (STCE), established in 2022, invests in a global index of companies that are involved in the crypto sector. The name of the ETF is a bit deceptive. While it holds shares in Coinbase, a direct crypto investment, it may also hold shares in PayPal and similar companies, whose business is related to crypto. Crypto is a small portion of its business.

Prominent Ethereum ETFs

Ethereum also sports a group of tradable ETFs; it pays to review the fund's information before investing.

The Grayscale Ethereum Mini Trust (ETH) invests in Ethereum cryptocurrency. It's a great way to invest in Ethereum indirectly while capturing its general price trend. You can trade options on this ETF. Because of high levels of competition, this ETF, along with other Ethereum-based ETFs, have low fees.

The iShares Ethereum Trust ETF (ETHA), established in 2024, is another reliable vehicle through which you can participate in the price trend of the Ethereum cryptocurrency. There are other Ethereum-based ETFs like the VanEck Ethereum ETF (ETHV) and the Bitwise Ethereum ETF (ETHW). ETHW invests passively in Ethereum and offers the ability to capitalize on the price trend of Ethereum's entire platform.

Some Quick Advice on ETFs

You can invest in cryptocurrencies and companies that hold cryptocurrencies, or those that do business in the crypto space indirectly through ETFs. You don't have to open a crypto wallet to trade ETFs if you have a brokerage account, and tax-related issues can be simplified through investing in ETFs. However, please read the fund's information thoroughly before investing, and consult the regional rules and regulations as they apply to crypto ETFs.

Chapter 7

Investing In the Building Blocks of Crypto

Cryptocurrencies have changed the way people think about money and how the financial system operates. It's likely that their growth as a storehouse of value, a payment mechanism, and as investments is just getting started. Yet, given that cryptocurrencies exist and operate in a totally digital environment, it offers the opportunity for further technological innovation. That means that their current and future operational and technological requirements of the cryptocurrency dynamic, its ability to exist as an asset class, requires the existence of a separate, but cooperative, ecosystem through which support and innovation of the cryptocurrency phenomenon can both exist, thrive, and expand. In other words, there would be no crypto without the support infrastructure that makes it operational (hardware, software, communication infrastructure such as the Internet and the electrical power) to run it all.

Think of Satoshi Nakamoto's great idea (Bitcoin) rotting on a white paper. Imagine trying trading crypto in a world where transactions take days, not seconds. That could be the reality if it wasn't for innovation and incentive in the tangible world of technology. There would be no operational exchanges, mining operations, wallets, trading apps, or other tools that we take for granted when trading cryptocurrencies without power companies to provide the power. These tools wouldn't exist without the technology and infrastructure companies needed to build, maintain, and operate the data centers where the mining takes place. As a result, this chapter is all about considering the diversification of your cryptocurrency investing via owning the stocks of companies that make cryptocurrency possible. To support crypto, it's necessary to hedge your bets on these other companies too.

CRYPTO MINERS STOCKS

Inside the Hardware That Houses Crypto

Once you get confident in trading crypto, you may consider exploring investing in crypto-related technology companies. A good place to start is with the stocks of crypto-related companies that produce the building blocks: the operational system and infrastructure required to mine coins and make transactions. Hardware is an all-inclusive term that refers to the machines and components of technology. So, while a computer program is software, the server or the computer that holds it is hardware. To understand the infrastructure of crypto mining at a practical level, this entry explores the ins and outs of the companies that mine the coins.

While it's important to remember that crypto mining is the process through which cryptocurrency transactions are validated and added to the blockchain, it's also important to appreciate that companies mining crypto may also have other businesses that are related to crypto or crypto mining.

BUSINESSES RELATED TO CRYPTO MINING

Mining itself requires a great deal of computing capacity (the ability to run multiple tasks rapidly), adequate housing (data centers), massive power consumption, and the ability to adapt rapidly to the evolving cryptocurrency landscape. Exploring "mining companies" is a mix of hardware, infrastructure, innovation, and how the company contributes to the demands of mining. Thus, in order to invest in crypto through companies that support it via their role in the infrastructure that makes crypto work, you should be willing to put in some time to research how and where they fit into the crypto landscape.

High performance computing (HPC) is achieved by assembling groups of state-of-the-art (cutting-edge) computer systems that perform complex tasks such as simulations, computations, and data analysis, which can't be done by ordinary computers. HPC computers have high processing power, extreme computational speed, and large memory capacities. Their original use was in drug design, weather analysis and monitoring, and scientific research. These are the computers that are used for the management of AI and crypto mining.

THE HARDWARE AND INNOVATION STORY

The early days of mining (circa 2009) were fueled by the central processing unit (CPU) model: the brain workings of traditional computing. The CPU model proved too slow, and graphics processing unit (GPU) circuits, initially used for gaming, came along. Between 2010–2013, innovation progressed rapidly. Programmable circuits known as field-programmable gate arrays (FPGAs) followed and allow for site-specific operations, increasing efficiency. Next came application-specific integrated circuits (ASICs): highly efficient, smaller semiconductors that are task-specific semiconductors and offer a high level of performance with low power consumption. All these circuits are the building blocks whose evolution has created the HPC phenomenon.

MARATHON HOLDINGS (MARA)

To give an example of a company related to the crypto business as a whole, take a look at Marathon Holdings (MARA). Founded in 2010, MARA is headquartered in Fort Lauderdale, Florida. MARA evolved from buying encryption-related patents. By 2021, it was reported to be an aggressive buyer of Bitcoin and Bitcoin mining equipment, which it powered through a joint venture with a coal-powered electricity generating plant in Montana, using the electricity to power an adjacent crypto mining center.

Over time, MARA has become one of the largest Bitcoin miners and Bitcoin holders in the world. Its market cap, as of August 2025, was just shy of $5.7 billion. Its listed holdings of bitcoin, at the time, were 50,639 BTC worth nearly $5.7 billion.

Knowing the Business Through the Earnings Call

MARA has a multi-segment business split into offering the hardware required to mine bitcoin as well as helping to run its own data centers. Its second quarter 2025 earnings call was a perfect example of how important this document is and why it's worth reading.

In the reported quarter, MARA delivered $238 million in revenue and surprised analysts with a profit of $1.84 per share compared to expectations of a loss. The results were fueled by increased Bitcoin production and aggressive cost management. They mined 25.9 BTC per day, which was 300 more coins compared to the prior quarter. Moreover, MARA transitioned to owning its mining sites, reducing electricity costs, and improving operational efficiency. They accomplished this by operating a mining center next to a company-owned power generation plant in Texas. Additionally, the company remained focused on its international expansion, cost cutting, and continued growth in Bitcoin production.

Marathon provides an excellent example of what you want to see when analyzing a company: rising revenues, better-than-expected earnings, operational efficiency, and continued expansion plans for the future. On the other hand, the market didn't think the future was bright enough, so the stock sold off, even as Bitcoin's price remained in an uptrend. That suggested a lack of belief in the company's future from the market's perspective, which is worth noting when investing.

Digging Into the Balance Sheet

Given that MARA's lifespan is less than twenty years, it's important to explore its balance sheet (the document that best exposes how good a job management is doing in running the company). The traditional approach is to match assets with liabilities. Yet, it's often a better approach to see how much cash the company holds and compare it to its debt.

In August 2025, the company reported $109 million in cash with over $2 billion in debt. At first glance, this ratio should sound an alarm, but a closer inspection shows that MARA reported $5.7 billion worth of Bitcoin in its coffers. So, if things got rough, MARA could sell roughly half of its Bitcoin holdings to pay off a catastrophic debt. In fact, it's uncanny that the company's market capitalization is almost identical to its crypto holdings. Still, based on the quarter's performance, for now, MARA is worth keeping on your trading/investing radar.

RIOT PLATFORMS

A Pivoting Concern with Hidden Promise

As mentioned in the previous entry, MARA is gearing its future business toward Bitcoin. However, this entry focuses on Riot Platforms, Inc. (RIOT), a company expanding its business model beyond crypto mining in order to diversify its income stream. Specifically, it's expanding its data center footprint with the goal of renting space to AI-related companies.

ABOUT RIOT PLATFORMS, INC.

Riot Platforms, Inc. was established in 2000 under the name Bioptix Inc. The company changed its name to Riot Blockchain in 2017; however, in 2023, it was rebranded to Riot Platforms, Inc. as its focus shifted more toward crypto mining. It currently operates mining data centers in Texas. Now, Riot Platforms is again adjusting its business focus to data center expansion. The stock's price record was over $3,000 in 2007, while its low was below $3 per share in 2020. In August 2025, the stock was trading near $12.

Finances

The details of the company's finances, based on its July 31, 2025, Q2 report, told the story of how the company is faring. The company's revenues decreased 5% from its prior quarter because its Bitcoin production fell as customers reduced their mining requests. Its earnings were up, but the increase was due to its Bitcoin holdings (over 19,000 BTC worth approximately $2.1 billion) rising in price, not because its sales or other income-producing avenues grew.

Riot had $300 million in cash on its balance sheet in September 2025 and its debt was nearly $900 million, but the Bitcoin reserves could cover a significant portion of expenses. Its cash flow showed nice growth measured on a year over year basis. Yet, the company admitted that although it mined more bitcoin for its own account than in the past, the fall in demand for mining from its customers hurt the bottom line and that in response, it would be accelerating its data center expansion project.

That's a red flag for sure, especially given the fact that the company's shares once traded above $3,000 and were once in the penny stock range (a stock that trades below $5). A further dive into the earnings report revealed that Riot's power costs were 77% of its mining expenses, and that's using its Bitcoin reserves to finance its expansion via agreements with Coinbase. Moreover, aside from its high-power bills, it spends up to $30 million per quarter in legal and other selling, general, and administrative expenses.

RIOT MAKING BIG MOVES

After all the negatives just mentioned, there's still a method to Riot's madness. What sets Riot apart from its competitors is its surplus power. Although available for use, Riot doesn't have enough business (enough customers or demand for its services) to use it for mining Bitcoin. Instead, it's attempting to get other companies to become tenants in data centers; it will build to their specifications and it would offer access to its untapped power sources.

Riot has an agreement with the Electric Reliability Council of Texas's Four Coincident Peak (4CP) program, which rewards miners for reducing demand during peak grid periods. This arrangement delivered $5.6 million in power credits to Riot in the month of June 2025. Compared to MARA, which faced penalties and operational disruptions in 2025, Riot has an additional revenue stream, and it can tout its electrical power management model to its data center clients who could benefit from Riot's ability to control their power costs. Riot also has aggressively invested in cooling systems for its data centers and has optimized hardware deployment so that more savings are built into the system.

Ultimately, with Riot Platforms, you're investing in a more diversified business model where crypto is being leveraged and where the income and revenue swings associated with the price of bitcoin are reduced.

Dig for the Details

When investing in any company (especially in crypto mining companies), it pays to dig deeply into their business models and balance sheet. By focusing on management's ability to execute and adjust its business plan and how it manages the ratio of debt to cash, you can gauge the potential future for profits.

THE REAL ESTATE, INFRASTRUCTURE, AND POWER ASPECTS OF CRYPTO INVESTING

Other Great Investment Angles

Real estate and power production are wonderful crypto-focused investments because you must have a location to put the data centers in which servers mine, secure the coins, and allow transactions to take place. These processes are very intense consumers of electrical power. So, this entry where crypto and the real world meet should be viewed from the relationship of electrical power and infrastructure and construction companies to cryptocurrency.

There are many traditional infrastructure and construction companies whose crypto data center businesses have grown since 2020. Many of them were involved in the cyclical construction business focused on building roads, bridges, and skyscrapers. After the pandemic, when commercial real estate crashed due to the work-from-home phenomenon, several of these companies transitioned to building data centers instead. Yet, there is one company that embodies the new wave of design and construction totally in tune with cryptocurrency and AI. This section describes the company Applied Digital (APLD) in detail, while simultaneously offering a simplified approach to investing in power infrastructure through an ETF.

APPLIED DIGITAL: AN ALL-PURPOSE DATA CENTER COMPANY

Applied Digital (APLD) is a pure data and crypto mining center operation servicing the HPC community, including AI. This company is a one-stop shop for HPC computing and AI data centers, as it builds the structures that house the servers and related components of the data center. This allows the clients to plug their machines into the existing prebuilt center. Originally incorporated as Applied Blockchain, the company was founded in 2001 and became a publicly traded company in 2022, while simultaneously shifting its business to designing, constructing, and operating data centers focused on AI and HPC.

Under the Hood

As of August 2025, APLD had a market cap just above $4 billion and is *not* a profitable company. If you look at its balance sheet, it's likely to spur some concern, with approximately $120 million in cash and nearly $700 million in debt. On the other hand, the company's sales are rapidly growing, and analysts expect at least 50% yearly growth by 2027.

APLD is purely a potential growth story, which could follow a similar trajectory to other tech companies, such as Amazon.com (which, over a few years, turned profitable and became dominant in its field). APLD has competition, especially from more established traditional construction companies, which have transitioned from road and bridge construction to data centers.

Thoughtful Operations Model

Here is what makes APLD unique: Its focus is purely on data centers. In other words, data centers are not a division of the company—they are the company. It's this focus on one business track that makes APLD attractive, given that the underlying business HPC and AI (crypto and apps) is rapidly growing. Additionally, APLD has several crypto mining and servicing companies as customers. And while crypto is a central part of its business, the company understands that the crypto business is cyclical and, to a large degree, dependent on the price of Bitcoin and Ethereum. So, it's targeting the other segment of HPC, AI, aggressively.

APLD's three operational data centers, in addition to several others that are under construction, are located in North Dakota. This shows wonderful forethought, as there is plenty of natural gas available to power the data centers thanks to the Bakken oil field. These centers attract potential customers, to whom power costs are top of their concern. Over the next few years, there's a likelihood of natural gas pipelines expanding to the areas where the APLD data centers are located, since there has been state approval for construction of pipelines to the data centers' locations. In addition, the company has streamlined its building process from twenty-four months to twelve to fourteen months, allowing it to deliver facilities to its customers faster.

In its July 2025 earnings call, the company beat analyst expectations with a much smaller-than-expected loss of $0.03 per share versus expectations of $0.14 per share. Then, in June 2025, the company announced a fifteen-year $7 billion lease contract with AI company CoreWeave (CRWV), which should work its way to both the revenues and earnings column for APLD.

Power Production Investing Simplified

AI and crypto mining are mega power consumers, which raises environmental concerns. From an investment standpoint, the regional nature of power grids would require an entire book to fully flesh out this potential investment sector. Thus, from a practical standpoint, it makes sense to consider an ETF as a practical way to invest in the power required to operate data centers.

A well-diversified sector ETF to consider is the Utilities Select Sector SPDR Fund (XLU). This ETF offers access to electric and water utilities, diversified power producers, renewable power producers, and natural gas utilities.

You can invest in this ETF both for short-term trades and use it as part of a diversified long-term portfolio approach. Utility companies often pay above-average dividends, thus this ETF may be used as part of an income-producing plan via its quarterly dividend.

INVESTING IN CRYPTO-RELATED SEMICONDUCTORS

Semiconductors Do the Heavy Lifting

Semiconductors are the backbone of the cryptocurrency ecosystem. A semiconductor is an electronic circuit component that is built around material that have properties between conductors and insulators. Semiconductors control electricity flow at rates between conductors (such as copper) and insulating materials (such as rubber). Semiconductors are attractive due to their ability to conduct electricity at various rates dependent on the addition of other materials to the mix (a process called "doping"). By mixing in other components with the base semiconductor, the speed through which the electricity flows through the circuit is adjusted and the circuit can be operated as an electrical switch. There are two types of semiconductors: intrinsics, which are the natural materials, and extrinsic, also known as "doped" semiconductors.

The latter category is the basis for computers, servers, mobile phones, and a wide array of electronic products used today. For cryptocurrency, these semiconductors (chips) are the brains and auxiliary components of the servers. These servers house software that allows for mining, trading, storage, and security, along with other processes required for the cryptocurrency world to work. In other words, without the chips, there wouldn't be any crypto, except on white papers. There are several bellwether companies in the cryptocurrency semiconductor space to consider: Nvidia, Advanced Micro Devices, and Bitmain.

NVIDIA

Nvidia is the world's largest semiconductor company, with a market cap of $4 trillion in 2025. Founded in 1993 by its current CEO Jensen Huang, with an initial investment of $20 million, it went public in 1999. Over the next two decades, the company grew tremendously due to the prowess of its GPU chips, which empowered the gaming industry to develop more sophisticated graphics and animation, thus enhancing the sophisticated nature of video games. They have since become the benchmark chip for crypto mining.

From 2000 to 2010, Nvidia developed a research platform known as CUDA to improve the GPU process. Then, Fermi architecture was developed, further enhancing GPU performance. By 2020, Nvidia introduced the A100 GPU for AI, and in 2024, it began producing AI chips via Blackwell.

Nvidia controls 92% of the GPU market. Its crypto chip–related revenue has been scrutinized by the SEC and is still hazy. Nevertheless, because of its crucial role in mining, it's worth considering as a crypto-related investment.

Investing In Nvidia

Nvidia (NVDA) trades on the Nasdaq exchange and can be a long-term holding in any portfolio. However, it can also be traded for short and intermediate periods of time based on technical analysis (the use of price charts and indicators to trade stocks).

To trade NVDA, you can use simple methods such as moving average crossovers. For example, for short-term trading, you can buy the stock as the price crosses above the twenty-day moving average and sell the shares when they cross below the average. For longer-term holding periods, you can use the fifty-day moving average. For long-term holdings, you can use the two-hundred-day moving average as a reference.

You can trade NVDA via single stock ETFs using the same approach as the shares. The same stock ETFs are leveraged, thus they should be reserved for short-term trading. The Direxion Daily NVDA Bull 2X Shares (NVDU) ETF trades at twice the underlying trend of NVDA shares. Thus, for every $1 up or down, NVDU rises or falls $2. The GraniteShares 2x Long NVDA Daily ETF offers the same type of leverage. Both ETFs follow the general price trend of NVDA shares, while leveraging the price as described.

You can also trade options on NVDA shares. Call options rise in price when the underlying NVDA shares rise. Put options rise in price when NVDA shares fall in price. You can set up sophisticated income-producing trades, such as spreads with NVDA shares. You can also set up speculative trades such as straddles, where you purchase a call and a put option simultaneously and you capitalize on a large-sized move where one of the two options rises in price in response to an event such as an earnings report.

ADVANCED MICRO DEVICES

Advanced Micro Devices (AMD) was established in 1969 and built a reputation as a builder of logic chips (field-programmable semi-conductors). The company went public in 1970, and by 1975, it was a contract manufacturer for Intel (INTC). Over the next twenty years, AMD became a competitor to Intel; in 2000, AMD introduced the Athlon processor, which cemented its place as a top-tier semi-conductor manufacturer. Over time, AMD made several important acquisitions and by 2006, it entered the graphics market. Since

2022, it has focused its growth on AI. It produces advanced GPUs used in crypto mining, and analysts estimate that crypto mining produces up to 20% of AMD's earnings. Ultimately, AMD is also worth investing in and the same general parameters described in the NVDA section can be applied, including the options strategies.

BITMAIN

Beijing's Bitmain, which is privately owned and specializes in chips used exclusively in crypto mining, is also worth keeping an eye on. While Nvidia's and Advanced Micro Devices's crypto mining activities are focused on GPUs, Bitmain produces application-specific integrated circuits (ASICs) built for crypto mining.

The company was founded in 2013. By 2017, Bitmain owned 75% of the Bitcoin ASIC crypto mining segment, reporting nearly $1 billion in net profits in the first half of the year. By 2018, the company ran into problems, as the drop in price of bitcoin reduced demand for its chips. In 2018, the company failed in an IPO attempt in Hong Kong, and in 2019, Bitmain tried to go public in the US, with no success either. In 2021, a power struggle between the company's founders led to changes in its management structure. Still, Bitmain continues to innovate, even introducing a new line of chips in 2024.

Look at the Price Charts

If trading Nvidia and AMD, you should become familiar with the price charts for both, especially their response to earnings reports. This type of event is often very profitable when setting up a straddle (a type of investment strategy).

INVESTING IN CRYPTO SOFTWARE

Thinking Practically

Semiconductor companies make chips that provide the operational backbone of the cryptocurrency ecosystem, and real estate provides lodging for the rigs. Meanwhile, crypto software companies wear many hats; they are better examined from usefulness of their functions. In other words, rather than viewing these companies in terms of the nuts and bolts of their software, it's best to explore how practical their software and apps are in terms of the services they provide and their ease of use.

Because blockchain is the lifeblood of crypto, at their core, crypto software companies are blockchain companies, where part of their business is participating in the operation of blockchain platforms. The other part of their business is developing apps that let users perform crypto transactions, including trading, banking, staking, fund transfers, purchases, and sales. There are many start-ups and privately held companies that design and market crypto-related software.

The potential for software design and implementation in crypto is vast, with multiple avenues for users at every step of development and use. This ranges from the creation of a token to its inclusion in a blockchain. Moreover, once a token is designed and fully operational, it has the potential to be applied to numerous crypto-related transactions. This entry features overviews of two large market capitalization, publicly traded companies where investors can utilize both short-term trading and long-term investing opportunities.

COINBASE GLOBAL, INC. (COIN)

Coinbase Global, Inc. (COIN) operates a full-service cryptocurrency exchange powered by an expansive variety of software, allowing users to perform numerous tasks. The company was founded in 2012 and went public in 2021. It was originally based in San Francisco; however, since 2022, it has functioned as a decentralized company with no physical central headquarters. In 2025, Coinbase was included in the S&P 500 Index, bringing a new level of legitimacy to cryptocurrencies.

The Coinbase Hacking Incident

Coinbase disclosed its earnings (and the hack) in an SEC filing in May 2025. The hackers asked for $20 million in ransom money, but Coinbase refused to pay and offered a $20 million reward for information to help catch the criminals. In addition, Coinbase informed all the affected users and offered to pay them back for their losses while increasing their security measures to prevent similar episodes (the hack was caused not by breaches of computer systems but by contractors taking pictures of customer information and selling them to scammers).

Coinbase provides a broad array of software-enabled services to consumers including trading, Coinbase Wallet for secure coin storage, and Coinbase Commerce for accepting crypto payments. It also offers its Coinbase Prime brokerage services to corporate and institutional clients, while also offering educational resources and tools to help users learn about and manage their crypto holdings.

What sets Coinbase apart from other companies, in and out of the crypto sector, is its CEO Brian Armstrong, who runs a tight ship. Perhaps the best example of Armstrong's leadership, and why the company is likely to survive and thrive over time, is how he responded to a hacking incident that cost 1% of the company's users an estimated $180–$400 million in losses.

Inside the Operation

Coinbase has a market cap of over $82 billion as of August 2025 and is well positioned to withstand difficult times. As of August 2025, Coinbase reported $7.4 billion on its balance sheet with only $4.7 billion in debt. Rather than using its cash, however, the company floated a $2.6 billion convertible bond offering in the summer of 2025. Convertible bonds give the company the option to turn the bonds into stock, which will give the bondholders an equity stake in the company. It's a smart way to raise money.

Moreover, Coinbase has delivered two years of over 10% earnings growth while growing its revenues at a faster pace (over 30% on a year-over-year basis). Together these metrics suggest the company is on a sustainable growth trajectory.

NU HOLDINGS

Nu Holdings (NU) is a São Paulo, Brazil-based digital banking company with operations in Brazil, Mexico, Colombia, the Cayman Islands, and the US. It's considered to be the largest digital banking company outside of Asia. Nu Holdings has a market capitalization of nearly $68 billion and sales of nearly $15 billion with revenues of $8 billion. Its net income is nearly $2 billion, and its sales, an important metric of future expansion, are projected by analysts to grow above 25% on a year-over-year basis until 2030.

Nu Holdings offers a wide array of traditional and crypto-related banking services to its customers, including multiple credit cards, prepaid cards, mobile payment solutions, and bill paying services via its banking app. It also operates Nu Shopping, a marketplace that allows its customers to buy goods through listed merchants, accepting both crypto and fiat currencies for payment. Nu Holdings also offers merchant transaction management services, insurance services, and a variety of loan services ranging from traditional loans to facilitating person-to-person unsecured loans. With each service, Nu Holdings can charge a fee. And with over 120 million customers as of mid-2025, the fees add up. Indeed, its rapid customer growth attests to the reach and acceptance of both digital banking and cryptocurrency.

One of the company's units, Nubank, is the third largest bank in Brazil and has extensive cryptocurrency-related products. These include cryptocurrency trading (including Bitcoin, Ether, and Solana), swapping crypto to the USD Coin (stablecoin), and sending and receiving crypto to and from their Nubank wallet.

Chapter 8

Taxes and Regulations

In the practical realm, anything that makes money is going to be taxed. Crypto is no exception, and because this currency is still evolving, the tax rules and regulations around the world are mostly still in progress. Therefore, just as anyone gets accustomed to the current crypto tax code, it's likely to change, and so, crypto users must be prepared to adjust via an accountant who is well versed in crypto or by a personal and dogged pursuit of the current rules and their evolution.

The IRS classifies cryptocurrencies as digital assets, which puts them in the property column for taxable purposes. They define digital assets as assets that can be stored, traded, bought, sold, or owned by electronic means. Furthermore, the IRS clarifies digital assets as any digital representation of value that is recorded on a cryptographically secured, distributed ledger (such as a blockchain or similar technological structure). It lists the following examples as digital assets: convertible virtual currencies and cryptocurrencies such as bitcoin, stablecoins, and NFTs. You can get full details at www.irs.gov/filing/digital-assets.

In this chapter, you'll find useful information about the evolving taxes and regulations for cryptocurrencies. Keep in mind that it's still early in the process. Thus, this, as with all other things crypto, will continue to evolve.

GENERAL TAX INFORMATION

A Complicated Endeavor

It took five years from crypto's birth (2009) to the US government to start taxing it. In 2014, via Notice 2014-21, the IRS classified crypto as property, making it subject to capital gains taxes. Thus, selling, trading, or using crypto for purchases are all taxable events. Because of the volatility in crypto prices, the IRS requires users to track (and record) fair market values for your cryptocurrency on the dates when the transactions were made.

CRYPTO AND FAIR MARKET VALUE

Fair market value (FMV) is the price of an asset on which both buyers and sellers agree to do business and close a transaction. The "fair value" concept assumes that both the buyer and seller are knowledgeable about the asset in which they are transacting and are behaving in their own best interest. Moreover, it's assumed that both buyer and seller are not acting under undue pressure and that both have been given a reasonable amount of time to review and complete the transaction.

For the purpose of reporting crypto transactions for tax purposes, you can calculate FMV based on the price listed on reputable crypto exchanges on the date of the transaction. If you traded the asset multiple times over a period of time, you could average the price over that period. You can also use information gained from a third-party valuation service specializing in calculating the FMV for cryptocurrencies.

IRS INVOLVEMENT

By 2017, the IRS became concerned at the lack of reporting regarding crypto-related taxable transactions and increased its enforcement actions against crypto users. In 2019, the IRS issued Revenue Ruling 2019-4, which addressed the effects and the required reporting of "hard forks" and "airdrops." An airdrop is a marketing tool used by coin developers where they distribute free coins to wallet addresses. A hard fork is a change in the programming of a blockchain, which makes the blockchain incompatible with the previous program.

The Importance of Recordkeeping

To comply with the IRS regulations, you must record the precise time and date when the taxable transaction was made and use reliable sources for the FMV figure you are reporting. As a result, you must keep meticulous records of all your crypto transactions. The maximum penalties for not paying crypto-related taxes may include $100,000 fines and up to five years in prison.

TAX TERMS IMPORTANT TO CRYPTO

Because cryptocurrency-related taxes are complex, it's important to have a good grasp of important definitions of key terms in the tax code. You can get full details at the IRS website (www.irs.gov/

filing/federal-income-tax-rates-and-brackets). The following are some important general definitions and details regarding tax rates, which will come in handy when you add your crypto finances to your tax filings.

Income

Income is money received for labor or services. Taxable income is income derived from wages, self-employment, or side jobs and similar venues. It also includes barter-derived benefits, royalty-derived income, and rent-derived income.

The rates for income tax (2025 inflation adjusted rates) on taxable income range from 10% for incomes of $11,925 or less, up to 37% for incomes above $626,351 for single filers. For joint filers, the rates are 10% for joint incomes of $23,850 to 37% for joint incomes above $751,601. You can review the full details here: www.irs.gov/newsroom/irs-releases-tax-inflation-adjustments-for-tax-year-2025.

Capital Gains

Capital gains are the profits from the sale of a capital asset such as stocks, bonds, a home, a business, or cryptocurrency. Short-term capital gains are the proceeds from assets held for a year or less. Long-term capital gains are the proceeds from assets held for over a year. Generally speaking, long-term capital gains are taxed at a lower rate than short-term capital gains.

Capital gains taxes may be different based on tax brackets and income level for the taxpayer. Single filers pay 0% on income up to $48,350. Joint filers (married couples) pay 0% on income up to $96,700. Capital gains taxes are 15% for single filers with income between $48,351 and $533,400. Joint filers share the same rate for incomes between $96,701 and $600,050. The rate rises to 20% for single filers with incomes over $533,401 and joint filers with income over $600,051.

AIRDROPS AND HARD FORKS

From a taxable standpoint, an airdrop is considered taxable income by the IRS. This action requires that you record the FMV of the tokens involved in the airdrop as ordinary income. If you sell the tokens in the future, the sale will be treated as capital gains. When you receive new tokens due to a hard fork, they are treated as ordinary income.

You report both airdrops and hard forks in Form 1040 (Schedule 1). If, for example, you receive tokens worth $2,000 in an airdrop, you report $2,000 of income on your 1040. If you sell the tokens for $3,000, you would report a $1,000 capital gain ($3,000–$2,000). If you sold the tokens in less than twelve months, the gains would be taxed as short-term capital gains. If you sold the tokens after holding them for longer than a year, you would be taxed at the long-term capital gains tax rate.

In both the case of airdrops and hard forks, it's important to refer to the FMV rules listed previously.

NONTAXABLE CRYPTO TRANSACTIONS

The Inevitability of Crypto Taxes

The act of owning cryptocurrency is not an automatically taxable event. As with non-crypto financial events, there are exceptions, and important details to know, which help you figure out whether any crypto transaction is taxable. First, it's important to understand the big picture when it comes to what taxable and nontaxable income are. The second step is to apply the general rules to crypto.

CATEGORIES OF NONTAXABLE INCOME

The IRS lists several general categories of nontaxable income. They all have their own specifics and are important to pay close attention to.

Gifts, Inheritances, and Other Related Expenses

Although gifts and inheritances are listed as nontaxable reports, there are some limits. In 2025, the gift tax exclusion is $19,000 per person; that amount is doubled for married couples. Inheritances are essentially tax-free, although an estate is limited by a lifetime exemption of $13.99 million. If you inherit property (such as cryptocurrency), it's valued at FMV at the death of the person from whom you inherit the property. Thus, you would only pay taxes on gains above the basis value. So, if you inherited a property with an FMV of $100,000 and you sold it for $110,000, you would be liable for taxes on $10,000.

Charitable contributions, gifts to spouses, direct payments for education/medical expenses (including employer-provided health insurance and most healthcare benefits) are worth considering as potential and legal ways to cut your tax bill. Ask your certified public accountant (CPA) about the details and documentation required.

Child Support

Child support payments are not taxable for the recipient but are also not tax-deductible for the party making the payments. Neither is reported on tax returns. Child support payments cannot be reported as earned income for tax credits by the recipient. The payers cannot reduce their income by the amount of child support payments.

Qualified Scholarships and Grants

Qualified scholarships and grants are tax-exempt if they are used to pay tuition and fees, including books and supplies required for coursework by a qualified student at a qualified institution. Housing/room and board expenses are not qualified. Qualified students are those who are enrolled with the documented intention of seeking a degree. A qualified institution is any college, university, post-secondary training program, or trade school that is eligible to participate in student aid programs designed by the US Department of Education. To qualify, these institutions must have existing and ongoing educational programs (curriculum), faculties, and student bodies. Always check if the institution is registered with the Department of Education and if the school issues a 1098-T Tuition Statement, which further documents your taxable status.

Welfare Payments

Welfare payments (government-provided social assistance) are not taxable. Thus, individuals who receive these benefits do not need to report them on tax documents. These benefits include Temporary Assistance for Needy Families (TANF), the Supplemental Nutrition Assistance Program (SNAP), and general assistance programs.

THE CRYPTO ANGLES

The IRS is quite specific about cryptocurrency, classifying it as property. Therefore, all the general tax rules regarding crypto are based on the principle that crypto is property. Knowing the ins and outs of these rules as they apply to crypto can be very useful in reducing your crypto related tax bill.

Being Patient and Harvesting Losses

The act of buying cryptocurrency and holding it (HODL) is a nontaxable event. The event becomes taxable when you sell the crypto for a profit. Remember that capital gains taxes, thus the timing of your sale, will affect the taxation of your crypto transactions. If you sell the crypto for a loss, it's not taxable. Indeed, you may reduce your overall tax burden via the practice of tax-loss selling (tax-loss harvesting). This sale allows you to reduce your tax liability by subtracting the loss from your overall gains in all your investments. You can reduce up to $3,000 per year on your ordinary income as an individual ($1,500 for married individuals who file separately). Any larger losses can be carried forward to future years. The benefits of this practice are void by the wash-sale rule. That's where you sell your crypto at a loss and then buy it back within thirty days.

So, let's say you sell a Bitcoin position for a $2,000 loss on September 1, but the market turns around and you like the price reversal. You can then buy back into Bitcoin on September 29. In that case, you can't report your initial $2,000 loss, as the loss is "washed."

Other Crypto Nontaxable Transactions

There are several transactions that won't lead to taxation of your crypto assets. First, the IRS won't tax your crypto transactions from one wallet into the next. This includes moving crypto from one exchange to another or from a wallet to an exchange.

Giving or receiving crypto gifts is not a taxable event, until you sell the crypto. If you sell for a gain, you'll pay taxes according to the prevailing rules. If you sell at a loss, you won't be taxed. Depending on your tax bracket and your personal circumstances, this type of loss can also be used for tax-loss harvesting. Crypto gifts up to $19,000 are not reportable. If you cash in the gift and make a purchase with the proceeds, such as using it for the down payment on a new home or car, there may be taxable consequences depending on the situation. Check with your accountant prior to making the transaction.

You can also give charitable donations using crypto, as many charities accept Bitcoin, Ethereum, and other tokens. The general rules of charitable donations apply. Make sure the charity is a 501(c)(3) organization and that it accepts crypto for donations. Keep detailed records. If your donation is above $5,000, you may need a qualified appraisal of the value of the donation.

Finally, child support payments are allowed if both parents agree to it. Depending on individual courts there may be special arrangements required. Some courts won't allow direct crypto payments for child support.

TAXES AND CRYPTO MINING

Taking Two Cuts from Crypto Mining Rewards

There's no escaping it: If you're a successful crypto miner, you are likely to pay taxes on your rewards, as the IRS considers crypto mining rewards as taxable income. Thus, your potential tax liability for crypto mining rewards initially depends on your income bracket and related particulars, such as how you decide to run your mining business and your expenses.

Thus, your income tax liability for crypto mining rewards may be anywhere from 10%–37% depending on your tax bracket and the amounts generated by your mining activity. Yet, given the amounts of money you may spend to set up a competitive mining rig, you may be able to deduct your business costs, and depending on how profitable your mining business becomes, it may be some time before the tax man sticks his hand into your mining pockets. For example, if you spent $10,000 to set up your mining hardware and you're spending $700 in rent at a data center or other facility, along with electricity and maintenance costs, you must figure this into your tax bill.

TAXABLE EVENTS IN CRYPTO MINING

There are two ways in which crypto mining may lead to tax payments, although it does not lead to double taxation. One, as stated before, is the taxable event that occurs upon the receipt of mining rewards. In this case, the IRS wants a cut of your rewards based on the market price of the day you receive them. In this case, if you receive a reward payment of 0.5% of a bitcoin on September 1, 2025, you will be liable, on your income statement, for ordinary income taxes based on the value of the coin upon the receipt of the rewards. Let's say that you receive $50,000 worth of rewards. In this case, you would be liable for the taxes on the $50,000 at that time (which would require that you make quarterly payments to the IRS).

The second way you may have to pay taxes on mining rewards is when you make specific transactions with the cryptocurrency you received as a reward payment. At that point, they are subject to all the rules of capital gains or losses, which means your tax liability, in this case, may be up to 20%.

The IRS capital gains rules for crypto mining are triggered by a disposal event, where you trade your currency for fiat, another cryptocurrency, or for goods and services. To calculate a capital gain or loss you can use a simple formula: Capital Gains or Loss = Fair Market Value (FMV) when you sell the cryptocurrency (the proceeds/the amount received when you sell the crypto) minus your cost basis (your original purchase price). A positive number is a capital gain. A negative number is a capital loss. A general reference to FMV is the value for a crypto currency listed on an exchange.

Here's how it may work. You're fortunate enough to receive $50,000 in rewards for a successful bitcoin mining operation. You then sell the bitcoin stake for $55,000. You recognize $50,000 in income and $5,000 in capital gains. Thus, your capital gains tax is only for $5,000, while your income tax would be based on $50,000.

HOBBY MINING VERSUS BUSINESS MINING

Before you report your mining taxes, you must decide whether your mining endeavor is a hobby or a business. If you report your mining as a hobby, you're going to miss out on deducting important expenses that could positively affect your overall tax return. These include electricity, equipment, maintenance, and possibly space rental costs if you're not doing the mining at home.

The IRS defines a hobby in terms of whether your goal is to make the activity profitable. Hobbies are described as leisurely activities designed for recreation, not for profit. That means that if you keep tight records, dedicate time and effort to the endeavor on a daily basis, and adjust the business toward profitability in the present and in the future, it's not likely to be considered a hobby by the IRS; rather it will be seen as a business, and you'll be liable for taxation as a business.

Moreover, even as a hobby miner, you may be liable for quarterly taxes on the mining endeavor. The triggers are:

1. If you expect to owe more than $1,000 in taxes after subtracting any withholding or tax credits.
2. If you expect your withholding to cover less than 90% of your tax liability for the present year or 100% of next years'.

The volatility of crypto prices may make it difficult to pay mining-related taxes. Thus, it's advisable to establish a reliable and separate cash reserve from your trading account (accessible pool of money) from which you can withdraw funds to pay taxes. One way to deal with the uncertainty of crypto mining–related taxes is to withdraw a portion of your rewards and convert them to fiat currency in order to have enough funds to pay their quarterly taxes.

If you decide to treat your mining business as a hobby, you'll report the rewards as "other income" on your Form 1040 Schedule 1, and this will limit the deductions. If you're running it as a business, you'll report the income on Schedule C and be able to deduct the expenses as you would with any business. You can get all the details on how to distinguish a hobby from a business here: www.irs.gov/newsroom/hobby-or-business-irs-offers-tips-to-decide.

Consequences of Not Reporting

Not reporting mining income to the IRS can lead to prosecution for tax evasion. The maximum penalty is five years in prison and a $100,000 fine. It's definitely worth your time to make sure you're filing properly.

LOWERING CRYPTO TAXES

Maximizing Your Tax Advantage Legally

There is nothing wrong with doing all you legally can to reduce your tax liability, especially with your cryptocurrency holdings and your mining operation. If you're able to work within the rules and regulations, you may be able to reduce your liability significantly, even to a level close to $0.

The first and most important strategy for reducing your crypto taxes is to be patient and consider holding on to your crypto assets for longer than a year. This means that you don't trade your crypto for fiat, trade one cryptocurrency for another, or use crypto to buy goods or services. If you do any of those things, you'll be liable for taxes.

ESTABLISHING A CRYPTO INDIVIDUAL RETIREMENT ACCOUNT

You can establish a crypto individual retirement account (IRA) through an experienced custodian such as Fidelity Investments. This would be a self-directed IRA that you can contribute to, along with your conventional IRA, as long as your total contribution does not exceed the limits for IRAs. For 2025, you can contribute a total of $7,000 to the combined IRAs ($8,000 if you're over the age of fifty).

If you choose a traditional IRA, your assets will grow tax-free until you begin withdrawal. In this setup, your taxes will be deferred, but you'll still have to pay them. When you begin your withdrawals (earliest IRA penalty-free withdrawals are at age fifty-nine-and-a-half), you would pay the current tax rate for the time based on your income bracket. The advantage to this approach is that your overall crypto holdings may be larger when it's time to begin withdrawals than if you paid the taxes up front. The potential disadvantage is that taxes may have risen by the time you begin withdrawals and your tax bill may be higher.

If you choose a Roth IRA for your crypto, then you pay the taxes up front and the account would grow on a tax-free basis. The advantage of the Roth IRA approach is that you can withdraw up to 100% of the total assets from the crypto account at age fifty-nine-and-a-half tax-free, as long as the account has been open for five years. Your best Roth IRA outcomes are likely if you work with an experienced tax advisor. The downside to the Roth IRA approach is that you pay taxes up front. That means that if tax rates drop in the future, you will have, in effect, overpaid. The flip side is that if taxes rise over time, you'll be ahead of the game.

HARVESTING YOUR LOSSES

Harvesting your losses is the practice of using losses to offset gains. Let's say you have a stock portfolio that has appreciated by $10,000 and you decide to cash it in. On the other hand, your crypto portfolio is down by $4,000. If you sell your crypto holdings at a loss, you would cut down the amount of taxes you would have to pay on your $10,000 stock-related gains. Harvesting tax losses is limited to $3,000 per year. Thus, in this case, you would reduce your tax bill by $3,000 for this year, but you would have a potential $1,000 that you could use for next year's return.

GIFTS AND DONATIONS

Up to $19,000 per year can be gifted without tax consequences to the person offering the gift or the recipient. If you decide to give cryptocurrency as a gift, there are simple ways to do so:

- **Crypto gift cards:** This method is usually safer when purchased through a reputable seller and the gift offered is a mainstream cryptocurrency such as Bitcoin or Ethereum.
- **Open an exchange account:** If you do this, you can simply gift the crypto to the recipient's wallet.
- **Gift via a paper wallet:** For this method, you write the key codes (the public and private keys that grant access to the gift) and hand a copy to the person receiving the gift.
- **Transfer the assets to a hardware wallet:** This is perhaps the safest way to gift.

No matter which method you choose, keep tidy records for taxable purposes. You may wish to consult your tax advisor before you gift crypto.

MOVE TO A CRYPTO TAX-FRIENDLY LOCATION

This may sound a bit dramatic, but if you're a crypto enthusiast and you're planning to move, consider a tax-friendly location. For example, Texas, Wyoming, and Florida have no state income tax and are crypto friendly, especially for businesses that transact in crypto.

Wyoming has over twenty laws that favor cryptocurrency-based businesses, while offering tax breaks on crypto mining equipment. Florida allows businesses to pay state fees with crypto. Texas has favorable electricity regulations, which may cut your mining expenses. Colorado, New Hampshire, and Arizona are also worth considering. Arizona does not tax airdrops. The least crypto-friendly states are New York, California, and Hawaii.

Crypto Tax-Friendly Countries

If you're looking to move to a foreign country, Switzerland, Singapore, and Portugal are considered the most crypto friendly. They feature favorable crypto tax schemes and clear regulations on crypto. El Salvador and the United Arab Emirates are also moving into the crypto-friendly country list. Depending on the country, you may find that crypto taxes are either very low or nonexistent. This, of course, is variable and clearly an evolving process. Thus, before making a major decision, you should verify the current and future status of crypto friendliness before moving to a new location, whether in the US or elsewhere.

STABLECOIN AND INTERNATIONAL TAX RULES

International Tax Rules Are Variable

As of September 2025, the stablecoin market was valued at $280 billion, growing from $200 billion in January 2025. So, if you own or transact with stablecoins, be prepared to pay taxes. That's because the IRS views stablecoins as property, the same as traditional cryptocurrencies. Thus, the same rules that govern traditional cryptocurrencies' taxes apply to stablecoins. That means that trading stablecoins, converting one coin to another, and receiving stablecoin-related rewards are taxable as income or capital gains as applicable.

The good news is that because the value of most stablecoins is designed to be close to $1, your tax bill may be negligible. On the other hand, you can include any fees incurred, such as exchange fees, during your stablecoin transactions in your tax reporting. No matter what your situation is, you still have to keep records and report your stablecoin transactions on your tax forms.

Therefore, when you sell your stablecoin for fiat currency, you must report any gain or loss incurred in the transaction. The gain/loss is calculated by subtracting the amount garnered at the transaction from the amount you originally paid. When you trade one stablecoin for another, it's considered two separate transactions. The first transaction is the sale of the first stablecoin, while the second transaction is the purchase of the new stablecoin. Both transactions are taxable separately. When you buy goods or services using stablecoins, you'll be taxed based on the fair market value of the purchased item (the item's value as listed in a credible source, such as an exchange, at the time of the transaction) minus the cost basis (what you originally paid for the asset) of the stablecoin you used for the purchase. Finally, if you get paid for goods or services with stablecoins, the transaction will be taxed as ordinary income.

Here are some examples of how this works:

- Let's say you buy $5,000 worth of bitcoin and then sell it when its value is $5,500 via a conversion to USD Coin. Because you started with $5,000 and ended with $5,500, your tax liability here is $500, which will be levied at the capital gains tax rate.
- If you receive $1,000 in Tether for selling an item to a customer, you must report the $1,000 as ordinary income.
- Now, if your Tether appreciates in price and you trade for DAI when it's worth $1,100, you must report the $100 gain, and it will be taxed as a capital gain.

Here's something to keep in mind. Let's say your stablecoin is collapsing in price and you've lost $400 in value since you moved into it. If you trade it in for fiat currency, you can report a loss on your tax form. It's rare, but it can happen. In 2022, the TerraUSD stablecoin collapsed and lost its peg to the US dollar.

You report your stablecoin capital gains and losses as you would your regular cryptocurrency gains and losses on Form 8949. You'll need to keep tidy and precise records of all your transactions. This could make for very tedious work, especially if you've logged in numerous transactions and used multiple wallets. The good news is that if you keep your transactions centralized, as on an exchange, the exchange may have software available that can populate the form for you.

To fill out Form 8949, you'll need:

- Details on all your disposal transactions—selling, trading, or using your stablecoins for buying or selling goods and services.
- Full details of the property you sold, the dates of purchase and disposal of the assets, the proceeds, the cost basis, and your gain or loss.
- To divide your transactions into short-term or long-term disposals for the purpose of capital gains taxation.
- To address whether you've documented and reported the transactions elsewhere to the IRS by choosing box A, B, or C in Form 8949, which refers to action taken on Form 1099-B.

Using an accountant will likely make all of this easier and may be the best bet to ensure you do these essential steps properly.

INTERNATIONAL TAX RULES

If you hold your crypto assets in foreign wallets, you'll have to take several steps to address the tax implications. Although each country treats cryptocurrency differently, there are some commonalities; for example, many countries treat cryptocurrencies as property and also assess taxes based on capital gains. The following countries all have different approaches to crypto:

- Switzerland has no capital gains taxes on crypto. It levies capital gains on a cantonal basis. A canton is a region of Switzerland (akin to a state). Some cantons levy significantly lower tax rates compared to others.

- Singapore treats crypto as barter and levies no capital gains.
- El Salvador has no capital gains on Bitcoin, which it considers legal tender.
- Portugal previously offered tax-free status for crypto. As of 2025, it now levies a 28% capital gains tax.
- Germany doesn't tax crypto that's been held longer than a year and has a €600 exemption for short-term gains. The capital gains tax for crypto held for less than a year is up to 45%.
- Japan has a 20% capital gains structure, which affects crypto.
- Denmark taxes crypto at rates ranging from 37% to 52%.
- China heavily regulates crypto. Afghanistan and Egypt prohibit cryptocurrency activity and use.

If you hold cryptocurrencies in foreign exchanges or wallets, make sure you check on whether you need to adhere to the requirements of the Foreign Account Tax Compliance Act (FATCA). If the assets are worth more than $10,000, you are required to file a Foreign Bank and Financial Accounts (FBAR) report.

Some International Advice

You'll really want to research whether a country you're interested in is crypto friendly before transacting inside their borders. Consider using an international tax expert/accountant if you're housing your crypto assets overseas.

OVERVIEW OF OTHER REGULATIONS AND USEFUL TOOLS

Crypto-Friendly Advice

It's clear that regulations that govern cryptocurrencies, their uses, taxes, and other important aspects of the realm are still evolving. Moreover, what's currently in place may be replaced by completely different rules and regulations. Still, while most countries allow the use of cryptocurrencies, most have at least some limitations on how crypto may be used. These can range from all out bans on the use of cryptocurrencies to lesser, yet meaningful, restrictions of crypto as an exchange medium. There are plenty of regional and international issues to consider on many fronts. And without this information, anyone who is just getting started could run into difficulties. This entry explores some overlooked issues that can have important impacts on your entire crypto experience.

Before diving in, consider why regulation is important. Primarily, regulations protect investors, or at least, give them remedies for Ponzi schemes and other fraudulent scams. They also provide a framework for security from hacks and data breaches. Additionally, they provide a buffer against market manipulation and other illegal activities while providing enough stability to the system and encourage established institutions to enter the arena.

REGULATIONS AROUND THE WORLD

In the US, there is a combination of agencies that regulate the crypto space. The SEC regulates initial coin offerings and crypto securities such as ETFs. The Commodity Futures Trading Commission (CFTC) regulates crypto derivatives (futures and options). The Financial Crimes Enforcement Network (FinCEN) enforces anti-money laundering (AML) compliance.

In the European Union, the Markets in Crypto-Assets Regulation (MiCA) creates a uniform set of rules to govern crypto assets, applying the rules to exchanges and custodians. It establishes uniform and enforceable rules for crypto asset issuers, service providers, and investors. Like the combination enforcement in the US, fraud and money laundering prevention/enforcement are its primary functions.

In the United Kingdom, the Financial Conduct Authority (FCA) regulates crypto firms for money laundering while offering restrictions on derivatives for retail investors. The Financial Services Agency (FSA) and the Australian Transaction Reports and Analysis Centre (AUSTRAC) respectively enforce Japan's and Australia's crypto activity.

China offers a difficult regulatory climate for crypto, which makes it difficult for crypto companies to navigate. In 2013, banks were prohibited from dealing in Bitcoin; ICOs were banned in 2017 and all crypto transactions were banned in 2021. As of this writing, China bans the ownership, trading, and mining of crypto. On the other hand, China encourages the use of its own central bank–issued digital currency, the digital yuan (e-CNY).

Still, there are pockets of embryonic action to be noted. For example, Hong Kong continues to develop a parallel legal and regulatory framework that allows exchanges to operate under these specific guidelines. Meanwhile, China continues to aggressively monitor China-based crypto transactions conducted overseas. Tech platforms in China are not allowed to offer or to allow the use of decentralized crypto wallets or decentralized finance interfaces.

THE EFFECT OF REGULATION ON INVESTORS AND TRADERS

Regulations affect exchanges by enforcing the Know Your Customer (KYC) rules, which require them to verify the customer's identity in order to prevent fraud and money laundering. KYC rules also regulate (and sometimes restrict) anonymous transactions, and they lead to taxation while encouraging investors to use regulated and registered platforms for crypto transactions.

Regulations also influence the credentialing of experts in cryptocurrencies. Here are some of the designations:

- **Certified Cryptocurrency Expert (CCE):** Individuals can go to the Blockchain Council and become certified by participating in 11 hours of coursework, which imparts detailed knowledge of cryptocurrencies and blockchain technology. The cost is $229. As of September 2025, a CCE accreditation is not required for employment in the crypto industry.
- **Certified Blockchain Expert (CBE):** Also offered by the Blockchain Council, CBE accreditation asserts that the recipient has a comprehensive knowledge of blockchain technology and is able to build and troubleshoot blockchain systems. To

obtain CBE accreditation, candidates attend a three-day course offered by the Blockchain Council with a variable cost. You pay $129 for a one-day course offered by the Crypto Valley Academy or consider other courses. As of September 2025, CBE certification is a valuable tool, as it gives the bearer a certain proof of expertise.

- **The Certified Node.js Developer:** Offered by the Global Tech Council, this certification testifies to the recipient's ability to build secure and scalable blockchain apps.
- **The Certified React Developer:** Also offered by the Global Tech Council, an accreditation offers participants the resources to build user-friendly crypto-related apps.
- **The Certified SEO Expert certification and the Certified Instagram Growth Expert accreditation:** Both offered by the Universal Business Council, these certifications are aimed at participants who are interested in providing expert marketing services to the crypto community.

Looking for a Career in Crypto?

The variations in the global regulatory climate, the emergence of certifications, and an increased focus on education suggest that cryptocurrencies may be permanent fixtures in the financial landscape. Plus, the potential for a crypto-focused career looks possible in areas ranging from programming and creating blockchain apps to marketing. That said, because crypto is constantly evolving, investors, traders, and potential workers need to be able to roll with the punches.

Chapter 9

What the Future Holds

It's not difficult to see a future where cryptocurrencies are fully integrated into the financial landscape. The bright side is that cryptocurrencies can offer opportunities to many who have been left out of the global financial system while providing convenience and lower costs to everyone. It's appealing to make financial transactions on a person-to-person basis, have a broader choice of investments, and access ways to accrue interest via rewards and crypto loans. Yet, it's also a bit of an uncertain future; there's potential for increasing levels of fraud and scams. Crypto also gives governments the opportunity to increase taxation, to influence and monitor populations during elections, or to have access to what should be private and personal transactions.

However, given that crypto is a self-adjusting complex system, what's certain is that there are periods of volatility balanced by periods of stability. As time passes, cryptocurrencies are becoming more ingrained in the financial system. Investors may see a broadening of the products and apps available to conduct crypto-based transactions and a potential expansion of employment opportunities for individuals in blockchain-related industries. This chapter looks at what the future might hold for cryptocurrencies and related ecosystems.

CRYPTOCURRENCIES AS RESERVE CO-CURRENCIES

A Double-Edged Sword

A reserve currency is widely held by governments and institutions as part of their foreign exchange reserves (foreign currency assets held by central banks including cash, bonds, bank deposits, and other government securities). Central banks hold foreign exchange reserves as a backup for liabilities in case their domestic currency suddenly loses value. In addition to currencies, foreign banks may hold reserve securities like treasury bills and bonds denominated in reserve currencies as part of their foreign reserves. Most foreign reserves are held in US dollars, as the dollar is seen as the most stable of all global currencies. As of September 2025, China is the largest holder of dollars as foreign exchange reserves. Other reserve currencies held by foreign banks include British pounds, euros, Chinese yuan, and Japanese yen.

An important aspect of a country's currency being seen as a reserve currency is its role in international trade. Depending on the source, the US dollar is used anywhere from 50%–60% of global business transactions. In September 2025, the most widely quoted range was 54%–57%. In 1999, the dollar was used in over 70% of global transactions. Moreover, a reserve currency allows the issuing government to borrow money more easily to fund its operations while also allowing the markets to tolerate higher fiscal deficits.

THE DOLLAR'S DILEMMA AND THE CRYPTO SOLUTION

It's clear by the decline in the use of the US dollar that its role as a reserve currency, although not terminally threatened, has been reduced. On the other hand, there are many regions of the world that don't have access to dollars but have access to digital assets/cryptocurrencies. At the same time, cryptocurrencies are plagued by the price volatility that's inherent to the realm. And that's where stablecoins come in.

Because stablecoins tame the price volatility of cryptocurrencies, the US has latched onto the use of cryptocurrency. The US government has even created a Strategic Bitcoin Reserve that holds Bitcoin, Ethereum, XRP, Solana, and ADA. Moreover, the GENIUS Act (signed in July 2025) requires stablecoins to be backed one-to-one by US dollars or low-risk assets (such as US Treasury bills).

As a result, the US has created a mechanism where the US dollar remains a reserve currency via its required backing of stablecoins. In addition, this creates a nearly perpetual need for US Treasury bills, which then allows the US government to continue to fund its deficits through their sale to issuers of stablecoins.

Where Things Get Hazy

The US government has created an entirely new dynamic by embracing cryptocurrencies, but there are potential consequences. For example, some projections suggest that exponential growth in stablecoins (with a market cap of $280 billion in September 2025) could lead to a market cap of $2 trillion by 2030. If this happens, it could cause the displacement of significant amounts of capital from the traditional banking system, with the potential to disrupt the traditional model of lending, which fuels economic growth.

Of course, there are ways to get loans via crypto. And by 2030, the whole process may be smoothed out. Yet, considering that all cryptocurrency-based transactions are potentially taxable as property (possibly as ordinary income or as a capital gain taxable transaction), this opens up a can of worms for those unaware of the potential repercussions of crypto transactions. You could make a case for governments to have converted the initial intentions of Satoshi Nakamoto (decentralized finance and anonymity) to a situation where cryptocurrencies are a vehicle for taxation, the perpetuation of government deficits, and the extension of the US dollar as a reserve currency.

An Increasingly Blurry Alliance

In a complex universe, there are no guarantees, and given the crypto ecosystem's penchant for surprises (good and bad), anything is possible. What is known is that the incorporation of cryptocurrencies and the rapid growth of stablecoins is moving forward at full speed. So, there are potential pitfalls created by a merger between governments, crypto companies, fiat currencies, and stablecoins that may never materialize. Yet, there is always the potential for a scenario, such as the 2008 subprime mortgage crisis or the 2020 pandemic, that could upend the fiat financial world, envelop the cryptocurrency ecosystem, and extend into the realm of stablecoins. If this type of scenario were to happen, and the markets decide that the traditional "flight to safety" response (buying US Treasury bills) isn't the solution to a developing financial panic, then stablecoin issuers might see the need to sell their US Treasury bills to cover stablecoin redemptions.

In this scenario, the sale of US Treasury bills would raise interest rates, just as central banks decide to increase the money supply (what they always do during financial crises). Then, fiat money would be printed aggressively as US Treasury bills are being sold in a panic, creating the potential for an inflationary crisis. This would all likely make the post-pandemic inflation debacle look tame.

Though there are benefits to cryptocurrency use, and stablecoins fill a huge need in the system by providing stability, there are still some unknowns. This is especially true when global governments are creating a financial world where the relationship between cryptocurrencies (especially stablecoins) and fiat currencies is increasingly blurry.

INTEGRATION INTO BALANCE SHEETS

Balance Sheets Make Things Valid

A balance sheet is a financial document that lists an entity's private, public, or government-related assets, liabilities, and shareholder's equity (in the case of a company). It allows interested parties (investors, creditors, customers, taxpayers, potential contractors) to gauge the economic status of the entity. Specifically, a balance sheet offers the opportunity to gauge the entity's solvency (its ability to pay its bills and its future as a going concern). The analysis of a private or public company's balance sheet should be evaluated differently than a government's balance sheet. Finally, there is one variable that connects both government and private/public company balance sheets: cryptocurrency. This entry investigates the emerging dynamic of crypto as a balance sheet component.

WHAT TO LOOK FOR IN A BALANCE SHEET

With a company, there are three important figures to consider in a balance sheet: assets, liabilities, and cash on hand. When reviewing assets, it's not as important to focus on the gross number as the details themselves—specifically, how much of the assets are inventory and facilities. If everything goes wrong, these are the most likely assets to be liquidated early in a bankruptcy or similar process. As a rule, it's useful to review the assets at a discounted price, since potential suitors are unlikely to pay full price when there is a fire sale brought on by a company with low prospects.

When viewing liabilities, note that, in comparison to assets, there is less likelihood that these would be discounted during a period of bankruptcy or liquidation. The most useful information on a balance sheet is how much cash/cash equivalents a company has and whether the amount is enough to cover the company's liabilities in a crisis.

Also, remember to review the details of the cash/cash equivalents column. For example, if a company holds over 80% of its cash/cash equivalents (CCE) in cash (fiat currency—especially major reserve currencies), it's a positive development. The next important sub-column is how much of the CCE is in liquid assets, such as treasury bills or money market funds. The final and increasingly important sub-column is the amount of cryptocurrency a company holds on its balance sheet. Because of the inherent volatility of crypto, it's important to note which cryptocurrency and how much of the crypto holdings are in stablecoins.

For government balance sheets, a similar process is warranted, with the understanding that a review of government balance sheets is not conducted with the goal of ascertaining the financial health of the government. Rather, a government balance sheet should be viewed with the goal of ascertaining whether the government can continue to function despite running what could be everlasting budget deficits and rising debt. Thus, it's a much more inexact process, in which analysis should focus on whether the government's currency is a reserve currency and whether that reserve currency allows it to sustain its current fiscal policy.

THE EMERGENCE OF
TREASURY COMPANIES

A treasury company is a company that deploys a significant portion of its cash into cryptocurrencies as a portion of their financial reserves. There are multiple reasons for this practice, including the diversification of their assets as a potential hedge against inflation and to attract investors.

Crypto holdings are listed as "digital" or "acquired intangible assets" on a company's balance sheet. By and large, as of September 2025, the majority of company crypto holdings are in the form of Bitcoin and Ethereum. Accounting rules require that the crypto assets be listed at fair market value. Companies must list the number of crypto holdings (itemized by each token) they have on their balance sheet while also listing if there are any restrictions to their sale and the methods used to calculate the cost basis for their crypto assets. Changes in the price of crypto holdings may affect a company's income statement, possibly impacting profitability. Good price appreciation of crypto could boost income, while the opposite is true when crypto prices fall.

Treasury companies are also required to provide adequate security and access controls to audit their crypto holdings, and to adhere to all pertinent regulations. As of September 2025, there are over 2,500 private entities (143 public and 302 private companies, along with exchanges and ETFs that hold nearly 1 million BTC and an estimated 3.7 million ETH).

A Close Look at Strategy Inc. (MSTR)

There's a new type of company doing business: the crypto treasury company, a company whose business is primarily owning and managing its crypto holdings. In some cases, becoming a crypto treasury company has replaced the original business enterprise.

The prototype crypto treasury company is software company Strategy Inc. (MSTR), formerly known as MicroStrategy. Originally, Strategy Inc. offered its clients enterprise-level software focused on business intelligence tools (business analysis/data mining software). The company went public in 1998 but nearly went bankrupt in 2000 due to an accounting scandal later settled with the SEC. While Strategy Inc. still sells software, most of its earnings are related to the price of bitcoin.

In 2020, the company's founder began to accumulate bitcoin with a $250 million cash purchase. Over time, the company has changed to a strategy where it issues convertible bonds (which can be redeemed for stock at a certain date), along with secondary offerings of its common stock and the sale of preferred stock to finance its ongoing Bitcoin purchases.

As of June 30, 2025, Strategy Inc. held 628,791 BTC at a cost of $46.07 billion and reported a total gain of $13.2 billion in bitcoin gains for the first six months of the year. More important, the company reported $14.03 billion in operating income from operations and $14 billion from unrealized gains (HODLing) of bitcoin with revenues of $114 million. In other words, crypto is the company's dominant business. The company reported $50 million on its balance sheet. Perhaps the most telling sign of this company's dependence on bitcoin as its central business, it offered analysts its forward guidance for the last two quarters of the year based on a projected price of $150,000 for bitcoin.

EXTENDED USE AS LOAN COLLATERAL

Crypto's Potential Role As Loan Collateralizing Assets

If cryptocurrencies are seen as property by taxing authorities, then they should be allowed to be used as collateral for loans. Thus, in what is an evolving dynamic, you can indeed use cryptocurrency holdings for collateral on loans, with some limitations. The acceptance of this practice is variable and is most often practiced in the realm of cryptocurrencies rather than through your local bank branch, although this is changing as some traditional banks are working on protocols to establish the practice.

GENERAL PRINCIPLES

When you want to borrow money and use your crypto holdings as collateral, you must have assets deposited on the platform through which you are scheduling the loan. Once you start the process, the first step is for the platform to verify your assets and current market value, then assigning you a collateralization ratio, also known as the loan-to-value (LTV) ratio (the total value of your collateral divided by your loan's amount). This leads to the calculation of the interest rate you'll be paying.

So, if the LTV is 40% and you deposit $100,000 worth of crypto, you can borrow up to $40,000. If you shop around and find a more favorable LTV ratio, such as 50%, then you could borrow up to $50,000 based on your holdings. Several factors can affect LTV, including price volatility (decreasing LTV), the individual policies of different platforms, and the type of collateral you use. Generally speaking, bitcoin and ether may have more favorable LTV ratios depending on their current price stability at any time. Stablecoins are increasingly popular as collateral as well.

The interest rate you may pay on a crypto loan varies by platform and may depend on the LTV ratio. For example, a higher LTV ratio may carry a higher interest rate. As with conventional loans, some crypto platforms use variable rates while others use fixed rates.

To figure out your monthly payment, take your interest rate and divide it by 12, giving you the monthly rate. Then multiply your loan amount by the monthly rate. Thus, if your rate is 12%, your monthly rate is 1%. With a loan amount of $40,000, your monthly payment would be $400. Plus, if your collateral drops in value due to market conditions, the platform will liquidate part of your collateral to protect the lender.

SETTING UP A CRYPTO COLLATERALIZED LOAN

When you're ready to take a loan with crypto as collateral, take these steps:

1. Sign up for your chosen platform and go through their Know Your Customer (KYC) requirements. This is where you provide information about your identity in order to meet the platform's requirements.

2. After you deposit your collateral (bitcoin, for example), the platform locks your bitcoin in a wallet where it verifies its value and assigns an LTV.
3. Next, request a loan. If accepted, the platform will issue a smart contract, which spreads the risk among several lenders or a centralized system (where the lender may be a single entity) and monitors your collateral as it issues your loan amount in fiat or a stablecoin.
4. Once the money is disbursed it accrues interest immediately. If the value of your bitcoin falls below the required level, you'll get a margin call and you either add bitcoin to the account or pay part of the loan to meet the requirements of keeping the loan active.
5. Once you repay the loan based on the agreed-upon terms (at the prescribed rate and on the prescribed date), the platform releases your bitcoin collateral.

Following these steps will set you up for success with the crypto collateralized loans, helping you achieve what you need to accomplish.

TYPES OF CRYPTO LOANS

There are various options available for crypto loans. As mentioned in the last section, there are collateralized loans. There are also crypto lines of credit where you set up an account but only borrow as needed and pay back only the amount you borrow plus interest. Interestingly, uncollateralized loans are available but are scarce. In this case, the lender evaluates your creditworthiness and lends you the money, usually at a higher rate than for a collateralized loan.

Then, there are flash loans. These are ultra-short loans that you borrow and repay with a single blockchain transaction. These are tricky to execute and thus require experience and expertise to pull off. Next you have stablecoin loans, which are based on stablecoins and are more stable than traditional crypto loans. And finally, there are fixed-term loans, which are similar to traditional bank loans and are set up to be repaid over a fixed amount of time based on a set payment schedule.

RISKS OF CRYPTO LOANS

As you would expect, there are risks associated with crypto loans and the crypto environment as a whole. These include price volatility of your cryptocurrency and that your loan may be liquidated due to sudden price changes. Always be aware of the finer points included in your smart contracts, as loopholes and general deficiencies in these documents could cause problems such as hidden fees and the potential for a hack, leading to losses.

There is always custodian risk. Make sure the platform you use for the loan is reputable. As always, there are interest rate risks with variable loans. Plus, regulatory issues may lead to unexpected outcomes.

TAKING PREVENTIVE MEASURES

There is no substitute for vigilance. It pays to monitor your collateral and LTV ratios to prevent a surprise loan liquidation. Diversify your collateral by using different coins. Keep up with the market so you're not surprised when the price of your collateral coin falls and consequences develop. If you're heavily leveraged, consider using futures and options to hedge your risk.

Some Red Flags with Crypto Loans

There are more variables that can affect a crypto loan compared to a conventional loan. They may be easier to obtain than conventional loans, but the risks due to price volatility alone make them something to fully consider before jumping in. Always do your homework before getting a crypto-based loan.

STABLECOINS AS THE BACKSTOP FOR FUTURE PAYMENT SYSTEMS

The Potentially Financial Equals of Fiat Currencies

The future of crypto is bright. Stablecoins are poised to solve a key set of issues with cryptocurrencies and the traditional banking sector, but the road ahead is still bumpy. Yet, when all things are considered, stablecoins may be significant players in the global financial system in the near future.

The major advantage stablecoins provide, and the number one reason for their attractiveness, is the ease with which international transactions can be completed. Thus, formerly complex activities such as remittances or business-related payments can be conducted faster and with lower costs. The downside is that, as with all crypto transactions, stablecoin payments are taxable events. Certainly, over the course of a year, these transactions may be washed out by business or other deductions, but they require meticulous recordkeeping. Plus, the current regulatory environment is likely to change in the future. The upside of more regulation may be increased consumer protection, especially from hacks and scams. The downside is the possibility of an increase in governmental scrutiny, which decreases privacy and increases the odds of some sort of legal issue with government regulators.

DOLLAR-BACKED STABLECOINS

The most user-friendly stablecoins are backed by fiat currencies—most likely the US dollar, as it's the world's largest reserve currency on a 1:1 basis. This process has been further eased by the passage of the GENIUS Act (2025), which establishes the regulatory framework with the goals being the facilitation of stablecoins as a payment system and the provision of consumer protections. The central tenet of the dollar-based stablecoin ecosystem is that the issuers must have US Treasury bills (or equivalents) on hand to back each issued stablecoin. The decisive step in the design, however, is the implementation of stablecoins into the blockchain, which gives them the ability to be transferred rapidly and seamlessly between those wishing to perform transactions, at a potentially lower cost than that offered by a traditional banking institution.

The adoption of stablecoins into the financial system is evidenced by the fact that as of 2025, some 70%–80% of crypto-based transactions on centralized exchanges involve stablecoins. Additionally, stablecoins are increasingly central to crypto-based loan systems. Moreover, stablecoins are steadily becoming entrenched in the conventional payment systems of emerging economies. Combined, most stablecoin transactions are via two major players: Tether's stablecoin (USDT) accounts for 60% of the activity and Circle's USD Coin (USDC) accounts for another 25%.

You can gauge the general tone of stablecoin transactions and the supply of coins in circulation on https://visaonchainanalytics .com, a website that is an industry agreed-upon benchmark for collecting this data. For example, measuring the activity for the prior twelve months, as of early September 2025, there had been nearly $41 trillion in stablecoin transactions involving over 296 million unique addresses conducting business. Plus, the stablecoin supply during the same period had risen from 159 billion to 247 billion stablecoins.

HOW STABLECOINS IMPROVE PAYMENT SYSTEMS

The current global payment system functions adequately, although there is room for improvement. Here's how stablecoins are contributing:

- Cross-border payments between institutions have to grapple with local regulations in more than one place, increasing the complexity of the transactions. Expenses increase, and this often creates a delay in the time for settlement, with the average cost of traditional cross-border payments being 2% for person-to-business and 2.5% for a person-to-person transaction. The average remittance cost was 5%. Transactions can take up to ten days, or more in some cases, to complete. In comparison, the average cost for a stablecoin transaction is about 3%, while the time to completion could be within minutes.
- Domestic payment systems may also be improved by lowering the intermediary fee charged by credit card companies, thus potentially lowering prices but more likely reducing transaction costs.
- AI's applicability to blockchains can also improve the efficiency of the global payment system by speeding up transactions and reducing transaction time.

It could take several years (a decade, perhaps longer) for the full acceptance of stablecoins as equal payment systems. Yet, their attractiveness and the speed at which governments are moving toward securing their status as "real money" suggest that, barring something very negative happening, it's more a matter of when than if.

POTENTIAL LIMITATIONS

Stablecoin use is increasing, especially as measured by transaction volume and the transference of capital from payers to recipients. Moreover, this rapid change of adoption seems to be happening faster in emerging economies, such as Brazil and India. Still, there are barriers.

For example, there are still many merchants who don't accept stablecoins for payments. Another is the on-ramp and off-ramp process for casual users. Those are the people that aren't using crypto for all their transactions and must transfer (on-ramp) funds into the selected platform for the transaction, and withdraw (off-ramp) the crypto, after conversion to fiat, from the platform. Certainly, you can use credit cards and debit cards as well as traditional bank transfers to complete the transaction, but that adds another step and increases the fees associated with the process. Over time, as stablecoin adoption increases, these limitations are likely to be reduced.

Platforms for Stablecoin Transactions

The majority of stablecoin transactions are conducted on smart contract–based platforms, such as Ethereum and Tron. Ethereum transactions are based on Tether (USDT) and USD Coin (USDC), while Tron transactions are mostly done with Tether.

EXPANDED TRADING PLATFORMS AND VEHICLES

How to Keep Your Crypto Moving

The traditional platforms for trading cryptocurrencies are the well-known exchanges such as Coinbase and Binance, which offer a broad range of services to users. These are known as centralized exchanges because they are controlled by a single entity.

Historically, centralized exchanges accounted for the majority of the cryptocurrency transaction volume. But as with everything in the world of cryptocurrencies, things often change, and change can be abrupt. So, it should not be surprising, that in mid-2025, the picture flipped and decentralized exchanges, where transactions are settled by smart contracts, overtook centralized exchanges in terms of trading volume. The reason is centered around the origins of crypto: the search for independence and anonymity. Thus, as centralized exchanges have conformed to government and regulatory changes, a portion of the crypto enthusiast crowd has shifted to decentralized exchanges. Moreover, as stablecoin use increases, these same enthusiasts may further increase the popularity of the decentralized exchange dynamic.

This change was further enhanced by the start of futures trading on decentralized exchange Hyperliquid, which functions on a platform-wide logic mechanism embedded into the blockchain platform. As this dynamic evolves, it may create two distinct playing fields: one where large cryptocurrencies, such as bitcoin, trade (centralized exchange) and another focusing on altcoins and stablecoin transactions (decentralized exchange).

THE EMERGENCE OF DECENTRALIZED EXCHANGES

In the past, decentralized exchange platforms were deemed slower and more complicated than centralized exchanges. Yet, that has changed, and decentralized exchange platforms are more competitive and starting to grab market share from the traditional exchanges, especially in trading volume for newly issued tokens. In September 2025, the top decentralized exchange platforms were PancakeSwap (Version 3) with 25% of the trading volume and Uniswap (Versions 3 & 4), with 7.7% and 5.4% of the decentralized exchange volume respectively. The total trading volume on all three exchanges combined was approximately $5 billion, a relatively small amount compared to what you would see on Binance, which had $174 billion on the same day.

In the world of traditional finance, transactions are conducted via an exchange and require a verification process by a clearing house. This leads to settlement in one day. In contrast, crypto trading can follow two distinct paths:

- Trading through centralized exchanges provides seemingly instantaneous settlement of trades via their internal ledgers. There is a settlement delay when users move assets off the platform into a bank account.
- Trading on decentralized exchanges requires using smart contracts that are deployed directly onto a blockchain (such as

Ethereum) to allow users to make direct transactions from their self-custodied wallets. Confirmation of the transaction usually unfolds in seconds.

Additionally, decentralized exchanges use specialized trading architectures, such as automated market makers (AMMs), which speed up transactions by taking the other side of the trade (providing liquidity) and by the use of central limit order books (CLOBs), which match orders between buyers and sellers. The spreads (the difference between the asking price and the offering price) are often better with CLOB setups, although they are labor-intensive on the IT side as they require frequent updates to keep them at their best operating levels. You can trade both spot and derivative crypto through decentralized exchanges.

PEER-TO-PEER PLATFORMS

Peer-to-peer (P2P) trading platforms are even further from the mainstream method of trading. P2P platforms offer users the ability to trade crypto one-on-one with other traders without intermediaries. This type of trading is attractive to traders who value privacy and are savvy enough to shoulder the responsibilities of the trading mode. P2P trading has two important features. First, it offers non-custodial trading where the participants keep custody of their own funds. Second, it simultaneously offers escrow services, which hold the funds until both parties fulfill their obligations.

Here's how P2P works:

- Interested users register on a P2P platform. Expect rigorous ID (KYC) verification requirements.
- Once registered, you create a listing, which specifies the cryptocurrency you're buying or selling, the amount of the intended trade, and accepted methods of payments. Specify any conditions for the trade such as minimum and maximum transaction amounts or other(s).
- Next, as the platform looks for a counterparty for the trade, your funds will be escrowed (reserved) by the platform. Once a counterparty appears, you will conduct negotiations about the price. Upon agreement by both parties the transaction is approved.
- Once the trade is confirmed, the escrow releases the funds and the transaction is completed.

The major advantage to this trading style is that you have control of your assets and have input into accepting any potential trade, while not having to deal with intermediaries such as banks and brokers. You can also trade across borders and have more privacy than through formal exchanges.

TWO P2P PLATFORMS TO EXPLORE

There are several popular P2P platforms to consider. Each has its advantages, although most of them offer the opportunity to trade a wide variety of cryptocurrencies and stablecoins including Bitcoin, Ethereum, and Tether, among others. This section explores a well-known entity-linked platform (Binance P2P) and an innovative international player (KuCoin P2P) that requires some nuance to operate, but which offers a wide variety of services.

Binance P2P offers the ability to trade P2P with the backing of the well-established platform Binance. This platform offers a chat function that lets the buyers and sellers communicate about their trade. It also offers low fees.

KuCoin P2P is known for its user-friendly platform. It also supports fiat currencies such as the US dollar (USD), the euro (EUR), and the Australian dollar (AUD). If your tastes run outside of the mainstream, KuCoin also supports other global currencies such as the Indian rupee (INR), the Nigerian naira (NGN), and the Russian ruble (RUB). In order to comply with SEC and CFTC regulations, KuCoin's use in the US must be through exchanges that partner with the company. Binance, Kraken, and Gemini are some of the operating US exchanges that partner with KuCoin.

There are many other platforms to consider. And as always, it's recommended that you do your homework before setting up an account in any crypto trading platform, including centralized exchanges, decentralized exchanges, or P2P platforms.

MORE ETFS AND MORE COINS

Giving You Further Paths to Explore

If you're interested in crypto as an investment asset but you aren't ready to pick an exchange, set up a wallet, and sweat all the details involved in tax reporting and other crypto-related endeavors, you can still use ETFs to trade the general trend of Bitcoin and Ethereum. Within the next few years, the number of crypto-related ETFs is likely to increase, as there are nearly one hundred crypto-related ETFs under review by the SEC as of September 2025, with the number likely to grow. This is especially attractive to those who wish to trade altcoins, such as Solana, Polkadot, and XRP via ETFs.

Moreover, the SEC continues to revise its crypto ETF approval process with the combined goal of speeding approvals while also increasing the consumer safety net regulations required to operate crypto ETFs. In July 2025, the SEC allowed qualified participants (large banks and institutions) to create and redeem ETF shares in kind. This process allows these ETFs to create new shares in exchange for the underlying cryptocurrency and to redeem ETF shares in exchange for payment in cryptocurrency. The net effect is to remove the conversion step from fiat to crypto and from crypto to fiat required to trade. It improves and increases the operating efficiency of the ETF via an easier settlement process.

WHAT'S ON DECK FOR ETFS?

Approval of a new ETF requires the filing of Form 19b-4 with the SEC by the proponent of the new trading vehicle. The companies who are filing for the listing of a new ETF are generically known as self-regulatory organizations (SROs). The filing of the form is a formal request for a change in SEC rules. In this case, the 19b-4 forms submitted by the management companies (SROs) is a request for the SEC to approve the creation of their new ETF. The SEC has up to ninety days to approve the submission of the form.

As of September 2025, the SEC had the following ETFs pending in different stages for approval:

- Solana ETFs under the management of VanEck, Bitwise, and 21Shares. The final approval stage was scheduled to begin in October 2025. VanEck is a giant ETF manager with ETF offerings in many sectors of the stock market. Bitwise is a US-based investment company specializing in crypto ETFs, including the Bitcoin-related Bitwise Bitcoin ETF (BITB) and Bitwise Crypto Industry Innovators ETF (BITQ), as well as the Ethereum-focused Bitwise Ethereum ETF (ETHW). 21Shares offers crypto-related ETFs like the ARK 21Shares Bitcoin ETF (ARKB) and the 21Shares Ethereum ETF (TETH).
- XRP ETFs managed by Grayscale, Franklin Templeton, and CoinShares are on the docket. Grayscale is a pioneer in the deployment and management of Bitcoin ETFs. Franklin is a giant manager of mutual funds. CoinShares is the leading European manager of digital assets.
- A Cardano-based ETF proposed by Grayscale.

- A staked Tronix (TRX) ETF is under review by the SEC. The fund's manager is Canary Capital. The ETF would include staked Tronix tokens to increase the yield available to owners of the ETF. The price of the ETF would be based on the price of Tronix on the CoinDesk Indices, minus fees and expenses. Canary Capital is a Nashville, Tennessee–based firm, founded in 2024, that offers digital assets to institutional investors including a crypto-based long/short fund, which combines both long and short crypto trades.

CONTINUED GROWTH IN ALTCOINS AND STABLECOINS

Meanwhile, new altcoins and stablecoins will continue to arrive on the scene for the foreseeable future. That's because the evolution of cryptocurrencies depends on its two guiding principles: anonymity (or at least increased transactional privacy), and convenience. So, members of crypto communities are always looking for improvement in existing coins and developers are always looking for ways to meet that demand.

New altcoins are produced via two mechanisms, a fork in an existing cryptocurrency or fresh from scratch. Both methods lead to similar ends: coins that are more efficient, perform specific tasks on a platform, or both. A fork is a change in the code for an existing coin, while new coins are based on initial coin offerings (ICOs), where the developer offers the new coins in exchange for existing coins. The proceeds of the ICO are usually deployed to improve the function and expand the reach of the newly designed coin.

More specific, intended uses of new coins include increasing the speed of transactions or fulfilling specific tasks within a platform. Let's say that platform XYZ offers gaming services to its users, but the processing in payments for game time is slow and the rewards received by the gamers are inconsistent. As a result, merchants involved and gamers are slowly leaving the platform, decreasing total revenue. This issue would prompt developers to first review the issues with the platform's problems in this regard. Developers would have to address the software and/or maintenance issues quickly, or they may choose to improve the existing tokens intended for gaming/to create a separate token, which would improve both problems.

The Fast Shifting of Crypto

The world of crypto is evolving and change is arriving rapidly. Keeping up can be overwhelming. As a result, a sensible approach when getting started is to stick with the familiar and time-tested assets. For trading and investment coins, that means bitcoin and ether, and for stablecoins, it's USD Coin and Tether. As you get more familiar with the space, you can expand your horizons.

SEAMLESS INTEGRATION INTO THE MONETARY SYSTEM

Looking Into the Near Future

The integration of cryptocurrency is ongoing and will likely continue for many years. What's clear is that it won't happen all at once, although at times it may seem as if the pace picks up. That's because cryptocurrency is a highly complex, complicated system, and so, it's important to understand the difference between complex and complicated.

Complex systems are systems with often infinite moving parts. A perfect example is an ocean, with fish, algae, protozoans, and other lifeforms all interacting with one another, creating a living system that continues to evolve. "Complicated" refers to a state of operation of any system or situation. Specifically, a complicated situation is one which is difficult to navigate.

Crypto is a bit of both, with lots of moving parts that sometimes get in each other's way, leading to a situation akin to a clogged pipe—where nothing moves. That's not a bad thing necessarily, as difficulties create the need for solutions, and solutions bring about change, which has the potential to eventually lead to progress. This entry explores some of the key parts of the crypto system, their interactions, and how the way issues resolve may shape crypto's future.

THE TRADITIONAL
FINANCIAL SYSTEM

The traditional financial system is composed of central banks, commercial banks, and other financial intermediaries. Central banks control the money supply, and the commercial banks distribute the money supply via loans while facilitating transactions between parties. Other financial intermediaries, such as those in the financial markets, provide liquidity to the system and offer investors the opportunity to develop their wealth, thus perpetuating the so-called "cycle of prosperity."

The traditional financial system relies on regulations created by governments to enforce the rules of the system. The centerpiece of the system is the fiat currency, backed by the legal tender promise of the issuing government.

THE DECENTRALIZED
FINANCIAL (DEFI) SYSTEM

Unlike the traditional system, the DeFi system was designed to operate with a different set of rules. Because they are digital currencies, and originally were not regulated, cryptocurrencies disrupted the "normal order" of the traditional financial system. The implementation of blockchain technology created a world where the transfer of value became part of a permanent record while still affording a relative level of anonymity to those involved in the transaction.

Furthermore, DeFi systems can function outside the purview of central and traditional banks because the blockchain is able to conduct transactions and keep perpetual records of each transaction independently. Moreover, tokenization and smart contracts offer a higher level of specificity of terms between those involved in the transaction without involving intermediaries. Thus, in a DeFi system anyone can buy and sell properties (tokenized or otherwise) without needing a broker or a middleman.

THE BIG DIFFERENCES BETWEEN TRADITIONAL AND DEFI

Unlike in the traditional system where central banks control the money supply, in DeFi, the supply of cryptocurrencies is purely dependent on the supply and demand for each coin. The central bank has no impact. Whereas stock and bond prices depend on central bank manipulation of interest rates and money supply, in DeFi, cryptocurrency prices may rise or fall based on the supply and demand for each individual coin. In other words, if the stock market is crashing because of central bank interest rate increases, Bitcoin's price could theoretically be in the midst of a major bull market.

CENTRAL BANKS MAY LOSE THEIR INFLUENCE

Here's an interesting possibility about what the future may hold. If the DeFi system were to grow to a point where more transactions take place within it rather than in the traditional system, central banks, and by default traditional banks could slowly lose control of the financial system. In other words, it is plausible that instead of logging on to, for example, Chase.com or driving to your local bank branch to conduct your banking business, you would access your crypto wallet and pay your bills from there.

If and when that happens, we would be looking at a totally different world. And while that may sound appealing to some, given that central banks have few fans, the possibility is daunting if the DeFi system is not regulated in a way that lets it function in the way it was meant to function, while still offering consumers and users a certain degree of protection.

WHERE THINGS MAY BE HEADED

This brings us to the potential future. Soon, regulators will be trying to put together an equitable system that allows DeFi to fulfill its promise—the provision of financial access to a wider variety of people around the world—efficiently, combined with enough protections to offer a safety net to consumers and users.

At the same time, large financial institutions see the writing on the wall, which is why big Wall Street firms and their international competitors are scrambling to offer ETFs that trade cryptocurrencies, and why traditional banks, such as JPMorgan Chase, have softened their stance against crypto and are beginning to offer crypto-related services.

Therefore, the take-home message is that cryptocurrencies are here to stay. They offer too much of an alternative to people who don't have access to financial services, and they are becoming ingrained into the world of investments. That governments are scrambling to develop regulatory regimens, and central banks are debating or implementing their own digital currencies is further witness to the reality of the situation.

Thus, the final frontier is when, where, and how the two systems (traditional finance and DeFi) will meet. It's possible that the two could find a way to coexist, with each system retaining its independence but acknowledging the presence of the other. Or there could be a merger of equals, where there is a seamless integration between both systems and buying groceries with bitcoin becomes a routinely performed task. The third (though unwanted) possibility is one in which the two systems clash and burn. In that case, the world would likely find itself in dire straits, not just financially but in just about every aspect of life.

The interconnectedness of crypto and the traditional financial system was highlighted on October 10, 2025, where more than $19 billion in crypto assets were wiped out after an escalation of the tariff war between the US and China. The markets stabilized after the US and China reached a temporary agreement. But the market volatility was rekindled when Federal Reserve Chairman Jerome Powell, told reporters on October 29, 2025, that the central bank was not guaranteeing an interest rate cut in December 2025. The selling in crypto resumed and bled into the stock market, causing further losses. As of mid-December 2025, neither the crypto nor stock markets had fully recovered.

Index

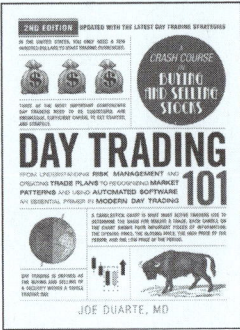